Jesus – Lord and Saviour

A. M. HUNTER

JESUS
Lord and Saviour

—••E)(3••—

William B. Eerdmans Publishing Company
Grand Rapids, Michigan

Library of Congress Cataloging in Publication Data

Hunter, Archibald Macbride.
   Jesus, Lord and Saviour.

   Includes bibliographical references.
   1. Theology — Addresses, essays, lectures.
I. Title.
BR85.H743   1978   230   78-19193
ISBN 0-8028-1755-6

Contents

Preface   vii

PART ONE

1   Reading the Bible (i)   3

2   Reading the Bible (ii)   11

3   Translating the Scriptures   19
    Appendix: Comparison of Versions   25

4   Interpreting the Scriptures   28

5   The Trustworthiness of the Gospels   37

PART TWO

6   The Kingdom of the Father   47

7   The Works of the Kingdom   58

8   Repentance and Faith   67

9   The Sermon on the Mount   72

10 The Books Jesus Read   78

11 The Meaning of the Cross   87

12 The Resurrection   98

13 The Person of Christ   108

PART THREE

14 The Holy Spirit   121

15 Christian Baptism 'I have a baptism to undergo'
    (Luke 12.50 NEB)   133

16 The Lord's Supper   138

17 The Christian Ethic   143

18 'Jesus is Lord' (Rom. 10.7; I Cor. 12.3; Phil. 2.11) 153

19 The Church and the World   158

20 Christian Paradoxes   164

21 The Secret of Eternal Life (John 17.3)   171

22 Hell, Purgatory and Heaven   177

Preface

This book contains some new things but also, though in briefer form, not a few themes which I have discussed in earlier volumes. Thus it summarizes most of my study of the New Testament over a period of some forty years and therefore constitutes, in effect, a kind of personal confession of my Christian faith.

I count myself fortunate that in my retirement my love of gospel and epistle has not suffered change or diminution, as I trust that this latest book does not bear too many telltale marks of my three score years and ten.

Once again I have to express my warm thanks to my friend and neighbour, the Rev. David G. Gray, BD (formerly minister of St Peter's Church, Dundee) for his careful reading of both typescript and proofs.

Ayr   A. M. HUNTER
August 1976

PART ONE

I

Reading the Bible (i)

Why should we read the Bible?

From time to time distinguished writers may be heard praising the Bible as literature, and suggesting that it is on a par with Shakespeare. They are right. The Authorized Version of the Bible made in 1611 is undoubtedly our noblest book of English prose – 'the most majestic thing in our literature and by all odds the most spiritually living thing we inherit'.[1] Yet, though this is a reason why, as we aspire to be educated people, we cannot afford to neglect it, it is not *the* reason why Christians account it the most important book in the world.

What then? Our forefathers liked to call it 'the good book'. Is it as a text-book on the good life that we should study it? Well, every thinking person is interested in the question of how best he may live out his allotted span. Is it because we have in the Bible the supreme text-book on morals that we ought to turn to it for guidance?

Again the answer is No, though now, as the children say in their game, 'we are getting warmer'.

Of course there is moral 'light and leading' in the Bible – for example, the Ten Commandments and the Sermon on the Mount. If it is light upon 'the good life' we are after, there is plenty – God's plenty of it – in the Bible. And yet this is still not *the* reason why Christians believe, with Sir Walter Scott, that 'there is but one Book'. What then do we find in the Bible which we find in no other book? We find in it 'the Word from the Beyond for our human predicament'. Dwell on this phrase for a moment.

When in time of calamity or bereavement men and women turn to the Bible, be sure that they are not seeking fine literature or even moral light and leading. What they are after is help from higher places. Overwhelmed by national disaster or by personal sorrow, perplexed by the mystery of life, they want 'a word from the beyond' to support them in their time of need. They want the assurance that in their suffering and sin the Almighty really cares – nay more, that he has 'done something about it', something worthy of a God.

It is just this 'word from the beyond' that the Bible, and no other book, claims to give. It declares not only that God cares but that once in history he came right down among us as a man 'for us men and for our salvation'. This is what distinguishes the Bible from all other books. It is, in the phrase used by W. Robertson Smith when he was on trial for heresy, 'the only record of the redeeming love of God'. In the Bible alone, as he said, we find God drawing near to men and declaring to us in Christ his will for our salvation.

Sometimes we say that it is the record of 'a progressive revelation',[2] a gradual self-disclosure of God to men as they were able to receive it. So it is: but when we use the phrase, we should stress the *noun* no less than the adjective; for the Bible is 'the literary deposit of the action of God', not revelation itself but the record of it – revelation being really God's actual interventions in history for our sake. In this sense we may say that God is the author of scripture.

We commonly call the Bible 'the word of God'. But in what sense is this true?

According to the Bible, Christ himself is the Word of God. In him 'the word of the Lord', which came to the Old Testament prophets, 'became flesh' – took human form (John 1.14). The Bible therefore is the word of God in so far as it promises Christ, testifies to Christ, mediates Christ –

but Christ, be it noted, as the incarnate grace of God, not merely (as some would have it) as the fairest among the sons of men. It would therefore be more accurate to say that the Bible *conveys* the word of God. This delivers us from the mistaken view, still held by some people, that every word in the Bible is the inerrant word of God, written down to divine dictation. God indeed speaks to us in the words of the Bible; and if we have learnt from it the idioms of God's speech – one important idiom in the New Testament being 'parable' – we may hear him speaking to us in our own situation and through the events of our time.

The next question is: Since we are Christians, not Jews, why should we not stick to the New Testament and leave the Old Testament to the Jews? This question has often been asked down the centuries. Not long ago so intelligent a person as the Duke of Edinburgh raised it with a friend of mine. Why do we reckon 'the Law and the Prophets' *Christian* scripture and bind them up in our Bible with the gospels and the epistles?

To begin with, because the Old Testament was Christ's Bible. In its sacred pages Christ found the historic record of God's gracious dealings with his own race and people and also the pattern of his own God-appointed destiny.

Next, because the Old Testament is the lexicon, or word-book, of the New. All the chief New Testament words like 'gospel' 'covenant' and 'kingdom' go back to the Old Testament and cannot be understood without it.[3] To throw away the Old Testament would be to throw away the key to the New.

Yet there is more to it than this. Jesus himself said that he came 'not to destroy the Law or the Prophets' (Matt. 5.17) – that is, the old revelation of God – but to 'complete' it. And the Old Testament is Christian scripture, both as history and as prophecy.

As history, because after recording God's creation 'in

the beginning', it tells the story of God's people Israel and his dealings with them through long centuries until, 'in the fullness of time', God sent the Saviour.

As prophecy, because through its prophets, the Old Testament promises and prefigures Christ.

This means that the Bible, for all its 66 books – 39 in the Old Testament and 27 in the New – is *a unity* – one story in two instalments – in which the Old Testament is related to the New as promise to fulfilment. 'These are they', said Jesus concerning the Old Testament scriptures, 'which testify to me' (John 5.39).

How do we best describe the story which the Bible tells? The answer is: as *a divine drama with three great crises*.

'Crisis' is a Greek word which literally means 'sifting', and so 'judgment'. According to the Bible, God visits the earth decisively in the great crises of history; and the 'Book of the People of God' contains three such crises which stand out as types of all lesser ones: the exodus, the exile and the dawning of God's kingdom.

It is making the same point in another way if we say that, for both Hebrews and Christians, God is the Lord of history, and that he is to be known from what he *does* in it. What we call 'revelation', i.e. God's disclosure of himself, comes through the events of history; and it is the business of the men we call 'prophets' to supply a commentary on the march of events and to tell their countrymen what God is saying and doing in these events. ('Prophecy' is the ability to get God's message – to recognize the significance of an event as 'revelation' – and to pass it on.)

And now to the divine drama with its three crises. Like a good play, the Bible starts with a prologue (Gen. 1-11), describing the creation and the fall of man, so setting the stage for the drama to follow;

The 'action' really begins in Gen. 12: 'Now the Lord said to Abram, Get thee out of thy country, and from thy kindred, and from thy father's house, unto a land

that I will show thee.' God tells Abraham of his purpose
to use him in order to bless 'all the families of the earth'.
(Here is the first hint that God means Israel to be a source
of blessing to all men.) In obedience to God's command
Abraham leaves the security of Ur of the Chaldees (an
ancient city on the Euphrates whose ruins have been
excavated) and goes out not knowing whither he goes.
(Here is the essence of true faith: it is a venturing forth
upon vision.) The Bible goes on to tell how Abraham's
descendants found their way, under Joseph, into Egypt.
There Pharaoh made them his slaves. The first great crisis
for God's people was beginning; its prophet and key-figure
was Moses.

There follows the story of the exodus. When their
fortunes were at their lowest ebb, God raised up Moses
to lead the Israelites out of their Egyptian bondage, and
at the Red Sea wrought a great deliverance for them.
'The Lord caused the sea to go back by a strong east wind'
(Ex. 14.21). Even if we explain what happened as a *natural*,
though very unusual, event, the Bible is clear that it was
an act of God, a miracle. The Lord had rescued his people
from their oppressors, and this rescue became a type and
promise of the still greater deliverance he would one day
work for his people.[4]

What followed is told in Numbers, Deuteronomy and
Joshua. Israel, rebelling against Moses' leadership, fell into
idolatry and was doomed to wander in the Arabian Desert
for forty years. When Moses died before reaching Canaan,
the land of promise, Joshua succeeded him; the Jordan was
crossed; and at Jericho the first Canaanite fortress went
down before them.

After the conquest of Canaan came the time of the
judges like Gideon, Samson and Jephthah: then of the
kings, first Saul, then David, then Solomon. When Solomon
died, his kingdom was divided for and against the house of
David. In the north, Israel began a new dynasty; in the
south, Judah kept David's sons on the throne. In the

northern kingdom, however, under King Ahab and his Phoenician queen Jezebel, the people began to forsake the true God and to fall into idolatry. It was then that the prophets Elijah and Elisha arose to recall Israel to her true allegiance. After them Amos and Hosea, the first of the *writing* prophets, warned Israel that their sins must bring down on them God's wrath. The judgment came in 721 BC when the northern kingdom (capital: Samaria) fell to the Assyrians who carried its people off into captivity.

There remained the southern kingdom of Judah. For the next hundred years, while Assyria menaced Judah also, prophets like Isaiah of Jerusalem arose to recall king and people to the true God and holy living. Then, some years later, Assyria itself was overthrown by Babylon whose menacing shadow fell ever more darkly over little Judah. It was then that Jeremiah, who saw the second crisis coming, pled in God's name, with king and people to submit to Babylon. They would not listen, and the crisis came to a head in 586 BC when Nebuchadnezzar, king of Babylonia, took Judah captive and destroyed Jerusalem and its temple (II Kings 24.25).

Had God's purpose for his people failed? No, said the prophets Ezekiel and 'Isaiah of Babylon',[5] God still has a future for his people, and the exiles will return. It seemed a thing incredible which nonetheless befell. Some forty-four years later (538 BC) Cyrus, king of Persia, who had defeated Babylon, issued an edict permitting the exiles to return (Ezra 1). The Lord had 'turned again the captivity of Zion' (Ps. 126.1).

The five ensuing centuries we may call the period of the 'Zionists'. The story, so far as the Bible tells it, is found in Ezra and Nehemiah: how the returning exiles, prompted by the prophets Haggai and Zechariah, rebuilt the temple and the city walls; and how, resolved to be a holy nation living by God's laws, they purified their worship and, in a passion for racial purity, prohibited mixed marriages with foreigners. It was in protest against this policy of

Apartheid that the books of Ruth and Jonah were written.

Alas, in their zeal to be God's holy people, the Jews forgot that, through them, God willed to 'bless all the families of the earth'; and their narrow nationalism brought its nemesis when one foreign conqueror after another put Israel under his heel. After Cyrus and his Persians came the Greeks under Alexander the Great; and after the Greeks, the Romans under Pompey; and save for a short spell of 'home rule' under the heroic Maccabees (when the book of Daniel was written) Israel remained a vassal to foreign powers.

The story of the people of God, which is what the Bible is all about, seems over, and the end disaster, and not deliverance. But this is to forget the magnificent 'forward-look' of the prophets. Though Israel may seem 'down and out', they remain convinced that God has a future for his people which will eclipse all the glories of their past. Deliverance will come, they say, when God finally brings in his kingdom (Isa. 52) and his Messiah (Isa. 9 and 11); there will be a new and mightier exodus (Isa. 35 and 40); a new and better covenant (Jer. 31); God will pour out his Spirit on all flesh (Joel 2); and all nations will share in his salvation (Isa. 45 and 66).

The New Testament tells how that time did come – the time of God's kingdom and his Messiah, of the new covenant and the outpouring of God's Spirit – and how the prophecies were fulfilled with the coming of Christ:

> God, who to glean the vineyard of his choosing,
>   Gave them evangelists till day was done,
> Bore with the churls, their wrath and their refusing,
>   Gave at the last the glory of his Son.[6]

That 'Son' was God's answer to the prophets. But he was more: he was the answer to all the unfulfilled longings of every sad soul in Israel. Think of all those who, like the psalmist, cried, 'Wash me thoroughly of my iniquity', of all those, like Job, who sighed, 'O that I might know where I might find God', of every earnest soul, like Saul of Tarsus, who tried by keeping of God's law, to find peace with him – but failed.

All these were crying out for a divine answer. God's reply was Christ. And still today, to all who cry out for cleansing from sin, or a solution to the world's riddle, or an assurance that death is not the end, it is the good news of the gospel that Christ is 'God's Yes' (II Cor. 1.20), his historic and living answer to their prayers, with them, as he promised, 'to the end of time'.[7]

NOTES

1. A. T. Quiller-Couch, *On the Art of Reading*, 1920, p. 126.

2. It has been said that a progressive revelation must have primitive beginnings, just as the finest of roses have dung about their roots. So it was in old Israel's story.

3. Also 'the Son of man' (Dan. 7) and 'the Servant of the Lord' (Isa. 42 and 53).

4. The idea of the new exodus bulks large in the New Testament. See H. Sahlin's essay on it in *The Root of the Vine*, pp. 81-95.

5. The 'Great Unknown', commonly called 'the Second Isaiah', who wrote Isa. 40-55.

6. F. W. H. Myers, 'St Paul'.

7. Here are ten important (sometimes only approximate) biblical 'dates':

Abraham	1700 BC
The exodus	1300 BC
David	1000 BC
Elijah	850 BC
The exile	586 BC
The return	536 BC
The Maccabees	160 BC
The birth of Christ	6 BC
The crucifixion	AD 30
The conversion of St Paul	AD 33

2

Reading the Bible (ii)

The Bible, we said, is the story of the people of God – a story in two instalments, related to one another as promise and fulfilment, a story best told in terms of three crises – the exodus, the exile and the coming of God's kingdom.

When we broke off, we had reached the last and greatest crisis, of which John the Baptist, 'a man sent from God', was the herald. It began in the reign of the Roman emperor Tiberius (Luke 3.1) when a young man from Nazareth appeared in Galilee announcing that the supreme hour of history had struck. 'The time has come', he cried, 'the kingdom of God is upon you; repent, and believe the Gospel' (Mark 1.15, NEB). Familiarity has dulled our ears to the sheer wonder of these words. What they mean is: 'The time of which the prophets spoke has arrived. The reign of God is no longer a shining hope on the far horizon, but a dawning and blessed reality! God has now begun to take effective issue with the world's evil. Turn back to God, and make this good news your own.'

It is with this crisis that the 27 books of the New Testament are concerned. We start with the four gospels which tell the story of Jesus the Son of God and the bearer of God's rule to men. Paradoxical though it sounds, what Jesus said and did from the time he entered Galilee till the time when he was crucified on Calvary and raised from the dead, *was* the inauguration of the kingdom of God. Jesus was indeed the long-promised Messiah or deliverer, but a Messiah of a quite new kind, a Messiah who must

11

tread the path marked out for the Suffering Servant of the Lord (Isa. 53), a Messiah who 'came not to be served but to serve, and to give his life as a ransom for many' (Mark 10.45: 'many' is Hebrew for 'all').

The high-lights of the story are familiar – his baptism by John in Jordan, his temptation in the wilderness, his ministry in Galilee with its preaching, teaching and healing, Peter's confession of him as Messiah at Caesarea Philippi, his transfiguration on a mountain top, his march on Jerusalem and the cross ...

What it means is that God is offering the blessings of his kingdom to his people through his Son the Messiah. But old Israel will not hear; and Jesus, calling twelve men to be his lieutenants in the work of the kingdom, founds the *new* Israel which is to inherit God's promises and be for the world what old Israel had failed to be – 'a light to lighten the Gentiles' and bring all men to the saving knowledge of God.

In an upper room in Jerusalem, on an April evening in AD 30, Jesus pledges his men a share in the blessings of God's 'new covenant' (or 'dispensation', Jer. 31.31f.) soon to be set up by his own sacrifice. Then events take their grim course. Jesus is arrested, tried, condemned, crucified, buried. When darkness falls on the first Good Friday, it looks as if God's great purpose, embodied in Jesus, has been finally defeated. Dead in his rock-tomb lies the Messiah on whom all the hope of Israel's redemption had rested (Luke 24.21).

But no, there is a most astonishing sequel. On the Sunday morning three women find the rock-tomb empty; the crucified Jesus appears alive to his followers, commands them to proclaim his salvation to all men, and, for their mission, promises them 'power from on high'. Seven weeks later, at Pentecost, the promise is fulfilled, the Holy Spirit falls on the waiting disciples, and the new people of God, the church of the risen Lord, goes forth from the upper room, conquering and to conquer ...

Reading the Bible (ii)

The *Acts of the Apostles* forms the *bridge* between the gospels' story and the rest of the New Testament. It tells how, in three momentous decades, Christ's apostles, or 'special messengers', filled with the Holy Spirit, carried the gospel from the holy city to the capital of the world, and how they founded little outposts of God's new people all over the Middle East.

Chief among them were Peter, on whom Jesus had promised to 'build his church', and Paul, the ex-persecutor, to whom the glorified Christ had appeared on the Damascus Road. There were many others, notably St John whose main life's work was done in Ephesus.

What we call 'the epistles' are the letters which the apostles wrote to their young churches when, as we say nowadays, 'they had problems'. Thus Paul's letter to the 'gormless Galatians' shows him as the champion of Christian freedom when his converts were being tempted to exchange the new grace and liberty of the gospel for the old fetters of Jewish legalism. In Romans he is the theologian, expounding God's cure in Christ for the sin of man, and laying down the principles of Christian behaviour. In I Corinthians he appears as the wise father-in-God counselling his converts how to live as Christians amid all the temptations of 'permissive' Corinth. In Ephesians, which is a circular letter, Paul's theme is the mission of the church as Christ's 'working Body' in the world.

Similarly, in his first letter, written with the help of Silvanus, St Peter urges his readers in Asia Minor to stand firm in face of Nero's persecution of the church. In his first letter St John recalls his readers in Ephesus to 'the Christian fundamentals' when faced with the outbreak of heresy. And so on.

These letters show how men sought to live as Christians in a 'hard pagan world', learning by experience the triumphant sufficiency of their faith, the glad reality of their love, and the radiant adequacy of their hope. The last book of the New Testament, which is all about the judgment and victory of God, rounds off the New Testament with a Hallelujah Chorus: 'And they shall reign for ever and ever'.

All this is the first chapter in 'church history'. It is the period of God's dealings with men in which we live. We live between the time when God inaugurated his kingdom with the coming of Christ and the time when he will consummate his kingdom in glory, make an end of evil, sin and death, and reward the faith and patience of his saints in another and better world.

This is the event of which John the Seer of Patmos tells in *Revelation*:

> I saw a new heaven and a new earth (21.1). They shall not hunger any more; the sun shall not strike them, nor any scorching heat. For the Lamb in the midst of the throne shall be their shepherd, and he will guide them to springs of living waters; and God shall wipe away every tear from their eyes (7.16f.).

Such is the story of the Bible. We Christians believe that in Christ his Son God has given us his master-clue to the riddle of history; that he is working out a gracious purpose for us and for all men; and that he will bring all things to a blessed conclusion. Accordingly, as members of Christ's church, we are called to witness to the salvation he has wrought, and by our work and worship, by our service and our suffering, to testify to all men whose we are and whom we seek to serve.

Is the story we have been telling true, or is it just pious fiction?

The first thing to remember is that the Bible never sets out to be an ordinary history book. What its writers seek to do is to trace the guiding hand of God in a series of events which befell a special people but had significance for the whole world.

The next point to seize is that many parts of the Bible which we who live 'west of Suez' tend to take literally, were never meant to be so taken, e.g. the stories of Christ's baptism and temptation. The Bible writers were orientals who used poetry, parable and even 'myth', in order to convey God's truth.

Does this mean that there is no hard, verifiable history in the Bible but only poetry and parable? On the contrary, it is rooted in real history, and often the spade of the archaeologist can confirm events, places and people mentioned in it.

Thus, clay deposits found at Ur of the Chaldees, Abraham's birthplace, testify to a great flood in Mesopotamia. Stone tablets from Amarna in Egypt refer to the Israelites' invasion of Canaan. Recently the Israelis excavated the royal city of Hazor whose king, Jabin, was defeated by Joshua. Archaeologists have found the quarries where King Solomon got the stones to build the temple. Near Jerusalem, at Lachish, have been unearthed letters written by one of his officers when Nebuchadnezzar was besieging the city. An inscribed cylinder alludes to the decree of Cyrus of Persia permitting the Jewish exiles to return from Babylon. In the 'thirties' of this century the long-lost Pool of Bethesda where Jesus healed the cripple, was rediscovered; and under a convent in Jerusalem was found 'the Pavement' on which Pilate took his seat when Jesus appeared as a prisoner before him. At various points the Dead Sea Scrolls illumine the background of the gospel story. An inscription from Delphi in Greece names the Roman governor Gallio who dismissed the Corinthian Jews' accusation against St Paul. By means of it we are enabled to date the apostle's arrival in Corinth to AD 50. Even Gallio's 'tribunal', or judgment-seat, has been laid bare. And so on.

But if the Bible is basically fact, not fiction, we must repeat that its writers were concerned not with chronicling the precise sequence of events but with tracing an unfolding purpose – God's purpose for his people.

The Bible therefore is an *interpretation* of history and

an *invitation*. As interpretation, it tells of the purpose for which the world exists, the nature of its creator, and his gracious will for men. And the Bible is an invitation because, having put forward this interpretation as the right deduction from the facts, it invites us to make it our own.

We come finally to the question, How should we read the Bible?

One wrong way is to begin at the beginning and plod right through it from Genesis to Revelation. Many people used to do this, wading through it as others might wade through Tolstoy's *War and Peace*. If you tried it, you would probably find the Bible a queer sort of novel, with of course many 'purple passages' but also many dreary deserts in between. Long before you reached Paul's epistles you would probably have given up in sheer boredom, and decided to read on *a selective principle* which would have been the wise way from the beginning.

Another wrong way to approach the Bible is to regard it as a scientific text-book, which of course it was never meant to be. You maltreat the Bible if you put, say, the first chapter of Genesis alongside Darwin's *Origin of Species*. The man who said that the Bible teaches you 'how to go to heaven, not how the heavens go' had the root of the matter in him. Science is concerned with *how* the universe works and how life has developed on this planet. The Bible is concerned with *why* there is a universe at all and such a thing as human life.

What is the main point of these opening chapters of Genesis? The vital words are the very first: 'In the beginning God created ... Gen. 1 invites us to contemplate the wonder of the world, to believe that God is its maker, and that he has given man a status in it different from that of other created beings.

So with the Garden of Eden story. 'Adam', observe, is Hebrew for 'man' – a human being. And the story of the Fall in Gen. 3 is a parable about ourselves. We are fallen creatures, and the story of Adam and Eve is the story of Everyman – of you and me. The Bible goes on to tell how God turned the man and the woman out of the garden. A little later (Gen. 6) we read, 'The earth was filled with violence, for all flesh had corrupted their way upon the earth'. And is not this unhappily the grim truth? If we want evidence, need we do more than look in at 'News at Ten'? Or into our own hearts?

What then did God do about it? The answer fills the rest of the Bible; but two lines from Newman's hymn sum it up:

A Second Adam to the fight
And to the rescue came.

What then is the right way to read the Bible? To regard it as 'the only record of the redeeming love of God' and to study it with all the helps modern scholars put in our hands.

This means, first, reading it in a good modern translation like the *Revised Standard Version* or the *New English Bible*. If the Bible is to speak to us, it must speak in language we can understand, and the plain fact is that the Authorized Version of 1611, for all its glories, is often archaic, obscure and difficult for the modern man accustomed to get his secular 'news' in plain and simple terms, with plenty of headlines.

How should we set about reading the Bible? The old way was 'a chapter a day' and many people still favour it. To help them, there are books (with titles like 'The Bible Day by Day') which take you through the whole of it from Genesis to Revelation, judiciously choosing an appropriate section for each day of the year, and perhaps adding short explanatory notes.

The other and (as we think) better way is to choose a whole book of the Bible and go systematically through it with a good modern commentary. (Of these there is an abundance, from the very simple to the very learned.) Begin, say, with the Gospel of Mark which is the earliest of the four. Follow it up with St John's Gospel which is, in a sense, the key to the first three gospels, commonly called 'synoptic' because they provide a common outline of Jesus' ministry. After this turn to the Acts of the Apostles and read how Christ's apostles carried his good news from Jerusalem to Rome.

Having started in the New Testament, now turn back to the Old and study one of the historical books, like I and II Kings. Next, tackle a prophet – the best to start with is probably Amos. Don't miss those two wonderful little books, Ruth and Jonah. Then study some of the great psalms, so full of the spirit of true religion, e.g. 19, 23, 46, 51, 90, 104, 139.

Now come back to the New Testament, and study a letter of Paul's – the best to begin with is probably Philippians. A word of warning however! Until you have a fair idea of what 'apocalyptic' is all about, never tackle Revelation without a good modern commentary – or you may end up a crackpot!

Make notes on what you study, think and pray about what you are learning, and try to discover what God is saying to you in it about yourself, your neighbour and the world. With every book you master you will find your knowledge increasing, your faith being established on firmer foundations, and yourself abler to give a reason for the faith that is in you.

Let the last word belong to John Wesley: 'Reading Christians,' he said, 'are growing Christians. When Christians cease to read, they cease to grow.'[1]

NOTE

1. For the ordinary reader who wants a Bible which supplies brief and helpful 'introductions' to each book and (at the foot of the page of text) the minimal necessary comment, we warmly recommend *The Westminster Study Bible*, Collins. The text used is that of the Revised Standard Version.

3

Translating the Scriptures

'If the Authorized Version was good enough for the apostle Paul,' an Ulster Protestant is reported as saying, 'then it is good enough for me.' If his assumption did him no credit, his loyalty to 'King James' (as the Americans call the AV) was beyond question. But 'good enough' for the ordinary Bible-reader today? – this surely is the question.

Three and a half centuries separate us from King James, and in that time not only has the English language changed, but we now have access to older and better manuscripts of the Bible, as our knowledge of the biblical languages has significantly improved. Thus a modern and accurate translation of the Bible is both possible and necessary. To be sure, in trying to make one, we cannot hope to match the literary splendours of the AV; but to any uncritical, diehard defenders of the old book, we may fairly suggest that a moving Elizabethan cadence may be a sorry substitute for a Bible truth obscured.

Obscured by what? Obscured by archaic phrases ('I do ye to wit', 'I was let hitherto' etc.), obscured by words which are still used but have changed their meaning (e.g. 'prevent', 'peculiar', 'conversation'), obscured also by the wholly forgivable failure of the AV's translators always to bring out the precise meaning of a Greek or Hebrew word or phrase.

Begin with the Lord's Prayer as many of us repeat it in church. 'Our Father *which* art in heaven'. Here is an archaism. Nowadays 'which' refers to things, 'who' to persons. 'Thy will be done *in* earth'. Here the true reading in Greek is *epi*, not *en*, so that we ought to say 'Thy will be done *on* earth'.

Now take as an Old Testament example Isa. 28.16. Here the prophet is addressing the people of Jerusalem faced with the menace of Sennacherib the Assyrian – the same who (in Byron's words) 'came down like a wolf on the fold'. According to the AV, Isaiah counselled his countrymen, 'He that believeth shall not make haste'. But was he really advising the faithful in Israel to be cautious and go slow? Turn up the *New English Bible*, and light will break: 'He who has faith shall never *waver*.' Or, as we might paraphrase the verse, 'He who really puts his trust in God shall never panic'. Isaiah was letting his people – and us – into the true secret of fortitude in time of national crisis – unwavering trust in God.

Now take an illustration from the Sermon on the Mount. In Matt. 5.39, according to the AV, Jesus commands, 'But I say unto you, that ye resist not evil'. Does this mean that the disciples of Christ must never resist evil in any shape or form? Does it mean that, when attacked by a foreign aggressor, a nation calling itself Christian must never resort to arms? Of course, it does not. These words of Jesus were addressed to his disciples, and what he was forbidding was retaliation in case of personal insult. The NEB makes this clear: 'Do not set yourself against the man who wrongs you.'

It was archaisms, word-changes, and imperfect translations like these which made British church leaders in the second half of last century decide that the time was ripe for revising the Authorized Version. Unfortunately, however, the scholars chosen for the task were given a very limited remit. 'Make as few changes as possible', they were instructed. In the event, when the Revised Version appeared in 1881, it disappointed the hopes of many progressive Christians and drew down on itself the ridicule of the ultra conservatives who said, 'The old is better'. Moreover, the scholars found the new translation over-literal, as they deplored the revisers' decision always to use one and the same English word as representing one and the same Greek or Hebrew word. (In any two languages very few words are precisely equivalent.)

Nevertheless, the first step, however faltering, had been taken, and in the next century the re-translation of the Bible into modern speech became 'quite the rage' in scholarly circles.

Time would fail to list and evaluate all the re-translations of the whole, or parts of the Bible made in recent decades by individuals or by groups of scholars, by Presbyterians like James Moffatt or by Catholics like Ronald Knox ...

The three which matter most belong to the last twenty-five years:

The Revised Standard Version (1952)
The Jerusalem Bible (1966)
The New English Bible (1970)

The RSV, as we call it for short, was an attempt to improve on the ill-starred Revised Version of 1881. Sponsored by the Churches of Christ in America, it was the work of thirty-two scholars (including Moffatt), and its aim was two-fold: (1) to embody the best results of modern scholarship as to the meaning of the scriptures, and (2) to express this meaning in English which could be used in public worship and private devotions, and which would preserve as far as possible those qualities which had given the AV its supreme place in English literature.

When it appeared, the RSV won quick and deserved acclaim, from both public and pundits. It was seen to have kept many of the well-loved phrases and the consecrated rhythms, to have eliminated most of the archaisms, and to be simple and idiomatic in its English style, except for an occasional 'Americanism' (e.g. 'Counselor' for 'Advocate' in the five sayings of Jesus about the 'Paraclete' in St John's

Gospel). Moreover, experience showed that it was excellent for teaching purposes, and that it successfully survived the test of public reading in church.

If further proof of its merits was needed, it came in 1973 when the three great sections of Christendom, the Roman Church, the Orthodox Church and Protestantism agreed to recognize it as 'the Common Bible', that is, the English version of the scriptures acceptable to all three. For the first time since the Reformation one complete Bible now has the blessing of them all.

While the RSV was in preparation, the Roman Church had been feeling the need for a new translation of the Bible which would keep their members abreast of the times and stimulate study of the scriptures. In fact, much original work to this end had already been done in the Jerusalem School of Biblical Studies. The upshot was the publication in 1966 of *The Jerusalem Bible*. It soon earned favourable reviews. There was general agreement that the translators had successfully rendered the Bible into the language of today. An added attraction was the provision of brief introductions to each of the books and, at the foot of the text, short – and unsectarian – explanatory notes. One matter alone provoked wide dissent – the rendering of the Hebrews' primitive name for God by 'Yahweh' (AV: 'Jehovah'), where the RSV had, more wisely, preferred to write, 'the Lord'.

Meanwhile the Protestant churches of Great Britain, following a successful overture to the Church of Scotland's General Assembly in 1946, had resolved to embark on a similar task. Plans were made and scholars chosen – the director of the whole enterprise being C. H. Dodd – with the object of producing a Bible which would make the scriptures speak in the idioms of the present day, so that anybody, picking it up, would not feel he was reading 'biblical English'. The complete New English Bible (including the Apocrypha) appeared in 1970.

'New' it was soon seen to be. Joseph now had 'a long,

sleeved coat'. The sixth commandment now read, 'You shall not commit murder'. The famous words in Ps. 90 now became:

> Seventy years is our span of life,
> Eighty if our strength holds.

Now the *Magnificat* opened, 'Tell out, my soul, the greatness of the Lord'. The first Beatitude was freely but rightly rendered, 'How blest are those who know their need of God!' Now the prodigal son, before setting out for 'the far country', 'turned the whole of his share into cash'. In Gethsemane Jesus said to his disciples, 'My heart is ready to break with grief; stop here, and stay awake'.

In the Acts of the Apostles and the epistles the story was the same. 'The saints' (of the AV and the RSV), which might suggest that they were all moral paragons, now appeared as 'God's people'. Peter's word to Cornelius, 'God is no respecter of persons', now read, 'God has no favourites'. The wind 'Euroclydon' which buffeted Paul's ship on his voyage to Rome became 'the North-Easter'. Paul's key-phrase (e.g. Rom. 1.17) 'the righteousness of God', which has a dynamic nuance, was translated 'God's way of righting wrong'.

Out, except in address to deity, went the 'Thous' and the 'Thees'. So too did the 'lo's'. Particularly successful was the NEB's handling of biblical monies like 'pennies' and 'talents'. Thus in the parable of Matt. 18, we are told that the Unmerciful Servant's debt to his master 'ran into millions', whereas his fellow-servant whom he refused to forgive, 'owed him a few pounds'.

Of course the NEB had its critics who complained that much of the old magic of the AV had disappeared. Of course it had, and of deliberate design. It could not be otherwise, remembering the remit given to C. H. Dodd and his men. The every-day English which they were charged to produce can never hope to rival the glorious prose of the Elizabethans. Simple beauty and occasional magnificence (e.g. II Cor. 6.8-10) they often achieved; but clarity and modernity (in the good sense of that word) were their appointed aims, and these, by general consent, they attained.

To sum up. Only people like the Ulsterman with whom we started will refuse to avail themselves of the light on many a dark passage provided by these three finer modern translations of the Bible. When we do our Bible study, or perhaps choose passages to be read in church or school, we should have them within elbow reach. If, after examination, we find that the AV is tolerably clear, let us stick to it. But whenever a modern translation can illuminate a 'murky' passage in the AV, or make a Bible truth come home more vividly, we should not hesitate to employ it.

One word more. In these days of soaring prices the ordinary reader (as distinct from the professional teacher of the scriptures) can hardly be expected to possess all three of the versions we have been discussing. If you and I were restricted to only one of them, what, in the language of the Consumers' Association, would be 'the best buy'? Our answer would be, the Revised Standard Version. And if we were asked to state our reasons they would be five. First, the RSV seeks to conserve, so far as may be, the glories of the AV. Second, it harvests the best findings of modern scholarship, erring, rightly in our opinion, on the conservative side. Third, for teaching purposes it is the most serviceable and suitable. Fourth, for reading in public none has more dignity. Finally, as 'the ecumenical Bible', it is the Bible of the future, the earnest and symbolical hope of the ultimate coming-together and co-operation of the long-separated churches of Christendom.

Appendix: Comparison of Versions

(1) Genesis 1.2

AV   The Spirit of God moved on the face of the water.

RSV   The Spirit of God was moving over the face of the waters.

JB   The Spirit of God was hovering over the face of the waters.

NEB   A mighty wind swept over the surface of the waters.

Note: in Hebrew *ruach* means both 'wind' and 'spirit'.

(2) I Kings 18.21

AV   How long halt ye between two opinions?

RSV   How long will you go limping with two different opinions?

JB   How long do you mean to hobble on one leg and then on the other?

NEB   How long will you sit on the fence?

(3) Psalm 34.5

AV   They looked to him and were lightened.

RSV   Look to him and be radiant.

JB   Every face turned to him grows brighter.

NEB   Look towards him and shine with joy.

(4) Proverbs 29.18

AV   Where there is no vision the people perish.

RSV   Where there is no prophecy, the people cast off restraint.

JB   Where there is no vision, the people get out of hand.

NEB   Where there is no one in authority (footnote: or 'no vision'), the people break loose.

(5) Hosea 6.6

> AV   I desired mercy, and not sacrifice.
> RSV   I desire steadfast love, and not sacrifice.
> JB   What I want is love, not sacrifice.
> NEB   Loyalty is my desire, not sacrifice.

> Note: the Hebrew *chesed* means 'Real love' on Israel's part to God, and the covenant he has made with them.

(6) Luke 17.21

> AV   The kingdom of God is within you.
> RSV   The kingdom of God is in the midst of you.
> JB   The kingdom of God is among you.
> NEB   The kingdom of God is among you.

(7) John 14.2

> AV   In my Father's house are many mansions.
> RSV   In my Father's house there are many rooms.
> JB   There are many rooms in my Father's house.
> NEB   There are many dwelling-places in my Father's house.

(8) I Corinthians 13.12

> AV   Now we see through a glass, darkly.
> RSV   Now we see in a mirror, dimly.
> JB   Now we are seeing a dim reflection in a mirror.
> NEB   Now we see only puzzling reflections in a mirror.

(9) Philippians 3.20

> AV   Our conversation is in heaven.
> RSV   Our commonwealth is in heaven.
> JB   Our homeland is in heaven.
> NEB   We are citizens of heaven.

> Note: here the Greek word variously translated is *politeuma*.

(10) Hebrews 11.1

> AV   Now faith is the substance of things hoped for.
> RSV   Now faith is the assurance of things hoped for.
> JB   Only faith can guarantee the blessings that we hope for.
> NEB   Faith gives substance to our hopes.

> Note: the Greek word here causing difficulty is *hypostasis* which, in Heb. 3.14, means 'assurance'.

4

Interpreting the Scriptures

Every preacher or teacher of the Word engages in 'exegesis', and is in some sort an 'exegete'. As in most occupations, some do it well, some do it ill. What is 'exegesis', and what the task of its practitioner, the 'exegete'?

Turn up *Chambers Dictionary*, and you will find the word correctly defined as 'interpretation, especially biblical'. What rules or principles should guide the interpreter of holy writ and, hopefully, save him from reading his own ideas into the biblical record and, if he preaches from a pulpit, perhaps making himself a public nuisance with his private opinions?

The noun 'exegesis' derives from the Greek verb *exegeisthai*, which means literally 'lead (or bring) out'. For the ancient Greeks is usually meant 'explain' or 'relate'. But in New Testament times both noun and verb were also technical terms for interpreting or revealing divine secrets.

This is how St John employs the verb in the profound Prologue to his gospel. 'The only Son, who is in the bosom of the Father', he writes, 'he has revealed him (*exegesato*, the aorist, or past, tense of the verb) – made him known.' The evangelist would have us think of Jesus, who is the central figure in the gospel which follows, as the 'revealer' or 'exegete' of the God 'whom no man has seen at any time'. The story of Jesus is the truth about God, the word 'God' spelt out in human words and actions.

Interpreting the Scriptures

As Jesus was the 'exegete' of the unseen Father, so Christian scholars undertake to 'exegete' the sacred records concerning what we may call 'the Christ event'. How do they set about their task? What tools do they employ? And what deserves the name of Christian exegesis? Their tools are those of what is known nowadays as 'historical criticism', namely, accurate knowledge of the biblical texts and languages (Hebrew in the Old Testament, Greek in the New) plus what the experts in history, geography, archaeology, philosophy and religion can tell us about Palestine and the Middle East generally in biblical times. And the first aim and endeavour of the exegete should be to 'bring out' the original meaning of what prophet or psalmist, evangelist or apostle, wrote.

But question: Is such 'historical criticism', by itself, enough when we are dealing with documents which, in the Christian view, record a unique self-disclosure of God in history? Is not something more demanded of Christian scholars who believe (in Robertson Smith's phrase) that 'the Bible is the only record of the redeeming love of God'?

Writing in 1911 about some New Testament commentaries sent him for review, James Denney,[1] that prince among Scottish New Testament 'exegetes', observed:

> The study of criticism has apparently blinded the commentators to the fact that the books on which they are writing are *bits of the Bible* – that but for that fact they would in all probability never have reached us – and that *the chief business of the commentator is to elucidate their significance as vehicles of revelation.*

Denney was posing our question. When, with the aids supplied by historical criticism, scholars have exposed the original meaning of a passage in the Bible, may they lay down their pens, contentedly believing their work done?

Seven years later, in his famous commentary on Romans, Barth answered with an emphatic '*Nein!*' When commentators have fixed the true text, accurately translated it into modern speech, and added linguistic and historical notes, all they have done is the preliminary spade-work. This but paves the way for the true end of exegesis – the exposing of the Word of God in the words of men, for our guidance and instruction in Christian life today.

This man Paul, Barth explained, evidently hears and sees something which is absolutely beyond the range of my observation and the measure of my thought. He knows of God what most of us do not know, and in his letter to the Romans he enables us to know what he knew. To impart this knowledge of God to us in our human situation should be the aim of the true exegete.

So Barth proceeded to turn Paul's letter, written, about AD 57, in a back street of ancient Corinth, into what somebody has called 'an express letter to the twentieth century'. Of course his book had defects on which his critics pounced. Yet Barth had attempted to do what many of his critics never saw as part of their task – to treat Romans as 'a vehicle of revelation' for modern man.

> Paul, as a child of his age addressed his contemporaries.... as Prophet and Apostle of the Kingdom of God, he veritably speaks to all men of every age.... If we rightly understand ourselves, our problems are the problems of Paul; and if we be enlightened by the brightness of his answers, those answers must be our answers.[2]

Critical exegesis is a 'must', but it is not enough. If the exegete's first task is to discover the original meaning of, say, a prophecy, or a parable, his work is not completed until he has 'brought out' its *perennial* significance. On the one hand, he must never bypass or shirk the patient study needed to determine the original meaning. If he does, he will be tempted to allegorize or, worse still, to resort to *eisegesis*.[3] On the other hand, as he is a Christian and what he studies 'bits of the Bible', he must not lay down his pen until he has related his chosen scripture to the message of God's grace in Christ, which is the heart of the Christian good news (John 3.16), and make it speak to our human situation.

To be sure, our Western world differs vastly from the world of the Bible, and proclaiming the Christian verities to men mistakenly conditioned to believe that science is the sole source of truth, can be a very challenging business.[4] Even so, Barth is right. Our deepest human problems are what they were in Paul's day, as no real changes have overtaken the two persons with whom we have to deal.

The first is Christ. Ours is a living and unchanging Lord, 'the same yesterday, today and for ever' (Heb. 13.8):

> And warm, sweet, tender even yet
> A present help is He,
> And faith has still its Olivet
> And love its Galilee.

Still today Christ remains the one 'true and living way to the Father' (John 14.6, Moffatt), who alone 'has the words of eternal life' (John 6.68). Still today, when 'the chips are really down' – when it is not an armchair argument but the existential question of a faith to live by and a person to follow in this queer, puzzling world of ours, who else is there but that Christ on whom our fathers and forefathers set their hope and were not put to shame?

Here in Christ incarnate, crucified, risen, exalted, and now, through the Holy Spirit, present and accessible to his people, is all that the troubled heart of man could desire – the assurance, through that ageless cross, of God's forgiving love for sinners, the promise and power of new beginnings for all who have failed, and a kingdom of God which calls us to service among our fellow men, and which is invincible and eternal.

The other person who has not changed is unregenerate man. Time may have changed his outward circumstance: the inside of him it has not. In spite of all his science, his higher education and his improved psychology, no more than his first-century counterpart can he cleanse that heart of his which, by the judgment of Christ (Mark 7.14-23), lies at the root of all his spiritual malaise. For this 'heart disease' there is but one remedy – what St Paul called 'the power of God unto salvation' – God's dynamic for saving men – and what Thomas Chalmers, looking at it from the human angle, named 'the expulsive power of a new affection'.

To apply this remedy to man's spiritual sickness, in words and idioms which will come home to modern men and challenge them to decision, is the task laid upon all who are called to interpret and declare Bible truth.

Now let us see how our exegetical principles work out in practice, starting with what is probably the best-known bit of scripture, 'the absolutely flawless story' (as Robert Bridges called it) of the Prodigal Son.

Our first task is to discover its original historical setting and 'thrust' in the ministry of Jesus. Happily this constitutes no problem. This parable, like those of the Lost Coin and the Lost Sheep, was originally a riposte of Jesus – our Lord's *apologia pro vita sua* – in his war of words with the Scribes and Pharisees who complained that he was opening God's kingdom – offering his salvation – to social outcasts and notorious sinners (Luke 15.1). But the title given it in tradition is wrong. In the story the chief character is neither the prodigal son nor his self-righteous elder brother; it is that wonderful father who broods over the whole story from first to last. For this 'pearl among the parables' the true and proper title is 'the Gracious Father'.

Moreover, the only explanation of the parable which makes sense is that the father represents God, the elder brother the Pharisees who had criticized Jesus, and the younger brother the outcasts whom Jesus had befriended. In the parable, therefore, God, by the lips of Jesus, declares his free forgiveness for penitent sinners, while at the same time gently rebuking those first-century 'Holy Willies', the Pharisees. It is a parable of the grace of God.

But how are we to make it speak to modern man and show him that the gospel meets his deepest need?

Let the younger son stand for all those who, 'fed up'

with the establishment and impatient of law and order, rebel against them and go their own wilful ways. Likewise, let the elder son stand for all unadventurous, conventional Christians who turn a cold, disliking eye on their rebellious contemporaries.

To those stay-at-home Christians – those 'dull, prissy paragons', as the prodigals might name them – who complain that they have always done what they should but have never had any 'bright lights' in their lives, the father of the parable (who is God) is saying: 'Son, you are always with me, and all that is mine is yours.' In other words, if you are in the elder brother's shoes, give God thanks for the blessings you so lightly take for granted, and be grateful that you have escaped all the heartache and hopelessness of your contemporaries.

And to our modern prodigals the Father is saying: 'You chose freedom, and I did not stop you. All the time you have been in the far country I have been worrying about you. And here I am, still waiting to welcome you home.'

For the abiding truth of the parable is that behind the drift and destiny of human things, and brooding over them in infinite compassion, is an almighty Father, and that, as the greatest returned prodigal of them all, St Augustine, put it, 'our hearts are restless until they find rest in thee'.

And the burden of the whole parable for us today? There can be a homecoming for us all because there is a home. The door of the kingdom which leads to the Father's house still stands open, as there is one who has died and risen to open it to all believers. Now it is 'Over to us!' The question which each of us must decide for himself is: 'Do we want to come home?'

Now, for an example from the epistles, let us take 'the great persuasion' with which Paul rounds off his exposition of God's grace in Christ to sinners, which is the theme of Rom. 1-8.

To begin with, let us paraphrase what Paul says: 'With

all these evidences of God's love before us, we Christians have nothing to fear. God the great judge is on our side, as his Son Jesus Christ, who has died for us, now risen and exalted, prays for us in heaven. So strong is God's love in Christ that no earthly trials and tribulations – indeed no forms or phases of being – can get between us and that love. Whatever befall us, we are held by a love that will not let us go.'

'Having Christ, we have all' – this is Paul's first point (31ff.). 'As Abraham did not spare Isaac, so our heavenly Father spared not the Son who shared his Godhead but gave him up to die for us all. Is not this our assurance that, along with this transcendent gift, God will provide for all our wants?'

The argument is from the greater to the less. Because God has done the first and greater thing – given his own Son for our saving – we may trust him to provide for all our needs. In other words, it is because of the cross that we are to be sure of the daily providence of God.

But may not our sins separate us from holy God? For his answer (33f.), Paul bids us think in law-court terms. The court is sitting: on the bench is God; the prosecutor is Christ; and the prisoners at the bar are our guilty selves, well knowing we have broken the divine law and deserve condemnation. But wonder of wonders! the great judge acquits us, and the prosecutor, turning advocate for the defence, has done everything to procure our pardon – has died for our sins, and now in heaven pleads our cause before the almighty Father. Down is the barrier our sin had set up between us and holy God. We are 'justified sinners'.

Yet, if our sins cannot now separate us from God, may there not be other things like suffering and adversity which can (35ff.)?

No man in this life altogether escapes them, and many seem to get more than their fair share of pain, poverty, persecution and danger to life itself. May not these seas of trouble so overwhelm us as to separate us from the love of God? No, answers Paul, who had himself run the whole gamut of suffering and persecution for Christ's sake, no circumstances in life, however hard or harrowing, need so sunder us. In all our privations and perils 'we are more than conquerors through him who loved us'.

Finally (38f.), Paul gathers up his whole argument in his 'great persuasion'.

We mortals stand fearful and unassured before the mystery of life, the malaise of the present, the menace of the unknown future and (if we dally with astrology) the possible malignity of the stars above us. Fain would we know what lies beyond the Great Divide whose name is death—

> Whether 'tis ampler day, divinelier lit,
> Or homeless night without;
> And whether, stepping forth, our soul shall see
> New prospects, or fall sheer, a blinded thing.

Having 'put his hand into the hand of God' as revealed in Christ, how differently Paul confronts the ultimate mysteries! Already (Rom. 8.11) he has proclaimed the immortal hope which is ours in the risen Christ. Now he declares his conviction that nothing in death or life, no supernatural being or force, nothing that now exists or ever will, no stars in their changing courses – in fact, no world of being invisible to us now – can separate us from God's love to us in Jesus Christ our Lord.

It is a truly tremendous affirmation of Christian faith. But why should we regard it as a Word of God for us today? Is it not merely one man's opinion and as likely to be mistaken as the next man's?

The answer is that it is not, and for Barth's reason which we quoted earlier.

This is not just another man's speculation. This man Paul knows more – far more – of God than the next man, or Barth, or any of us. In him, as in his fellow apostles (see I Cor. 2), the living Christ, through the Holy Spirit, interprets his 'finished' work as truly as in his life-time Christ sought to interpret his 'unfinished' work, so that Paul can justly claim, 'We have the mind of Christ', that is, the 'intention' of Christ, which is God's 'intention', his loving will and purpose for men.

Romans 8.31-39 is therefore a Word of God not only for daily living but for that time when we come face to face with 'the last enemy'. It is the Word of God because it rests on the redeeming work of Christ – Christ crucified for our sins, Christ risen from the dead, Christ now in heaven and pleading for us, nay more, Christ now at work in us, through the Holy Spirit, and flooding our hearts with the love of God.

To awaken and create, to foster and feed, such victorious faith in human hearts today – should not this be the aim and end of any exegesis worthy to be called Christian?

NOTES

1. William R. Nicoll (ed.), *Letters of Principal James Denney to W. Robertson Nicoll*, 1920, p. 171.
2. *The Epistle to the Romans*, Preface to the first edition 1918, ET 1933, Oxford University Press 1968 edition, p. 1.
3. That is, reading one's own ideas into the text.
4. On this challenge see Dr A. C. Craig's splendid *Preaching in a Scientific Age*, SCM Press 1954.

5

The Trustworthiness
of the Gospels

'It's gospel truth', we say, meaning that our words are to be trusted. But can we trust the gospels? No books in the world have been subjected to such rigorous criticism as these four. How have they stood up to this long sifting and testing by the critics?

On this question it may fairly be said that men fall into three classes. At opposite poles stand two groups: on the one hand, the 'fundamentalists' who, in face of all criticism, still bravely hold fast their belief in the verbal inspiration and inerrancy of the gospels; on the other, the out-and-out sceptics who deny them any historical value. Between fundamentalists and sceptics are ranged a great majority who, if their opinion were taken, would probably agree with John Stuart Mill:

> It is of no use to say that Christ as exhibited in the Gospels is not historical, or that we do not know how much of what is admirable has been super-added by the tradition of his followers. Who among his followers, or among their proselytes, was capable of inventing the sayings ascribed to Jesus or of imagining the life and character revealed in the Gospels?

Does this verdict still remain the most reasonable one today?

As in other important enquiries, the first step in arriving at the truth is to ask the right question. So let us rephrase our opening one to read: 'Can we trust the gospels for the things which really matter for Christian faith?' And, remembering Thomas Hardy's counsel that 'if way to the better there be, it exacts a full look at the worst', let us start with the sceptics, among whom Hardy himself was to be numbered.

It was early last century, in Germany, with a man called D. F. Strauss, that serious questioning of the gospels' historicity really began. Today it continues in the work of another group of German scholars led by Rudolf Bultmann. These scholars, known as the 'form critics', seek to study and evaluate the 'forms' which they think the oral tradition about Jesus took before it was set down in writing in our canonical gospels. Bultmann's own conclusion – so extreme that his close followers are now disavowing it – is that the gospels are so shot through with the beliefs of the early church that what they yield us is 'the Christ of faith', not 'the Jesus of history' – Jesus as he really was. To put it another way, the evangelists did not really know the difference between the pre-resurrection situation and the post-resurrection one.

This 'way-out' view most British scholars, with native commonsense, firmly and rightly repudiate. If it were true, they say, how very odd it is that Mark, the earliest gospel, lends it so little support! Were Bultmann right, why is not Mark's Gospel shot through with the Christian doctrines which St Paul writing, in AD 57, to the Christians in Rome (Mark's Gospel was written in Rome about a decade later), could assume he held in common with his readers? Why does not St Mark enlarge, as St Paul does in Romans, on how Christ might be appropriated by dying and rising with him in baptism (Rom. 6.1ff.), or on the Holy Spirit as the divine dynamic of the new life (Rom. 8), or on being incorporated into Christ's Body, the church (Rom. 12.3ff.)? This question Bultmann and his men fail to answer.

'But', they may rejoin, 'never forget that a generation

separates Mark's Gospel from the events it records. Here surely there was ample time for the truth about Jesus to become distorted.' But is this really a telling objection? Is it not familiar experience that over a period of thirty or so years a man of sixty or seventy (as John Mark must have been when writing) will better remember events which happened a generation earlier than much more recent ones? (Anyone who was an adult between 1939 and 1945 has little difficulty today in remembering the salient events of that time and their general sequence: Chamberlain's declaration of war, Dunkirk, Pearl Harbour, Alamein, VE Day etc.).

Now if John Mark, a native of Jerusalem where his mother's house was a rendezvous for the earliest Christians (Acts 12.12), had worked closely with Peter and, as is credibly reported, had served, when required, as his 'interpreter', he must – unless he was an unconscionable dullard – have remembered the main facts about Jesus and been able to quote many of his memorable sayings.

To this argument for the historical value of the earliest gospel we may add five more for the general reliability of the four.

To begin with, the earliest Christians who were all Jews had a care for the faithful tradition (i.e. handing-on) of their Lord's work and words. To us, the word 'tradition' suggests something unfixed and uncertain. For the Jews, tradition was *the* way of preserving what their great teachers said and did. Nor was it unreliable because they had been taught and trained to remember, as we today, who rely so much on the printed word, have not. Moreover, we know that within about twenty years of the crucifixion (probable year AD 30) they had put together a connected account of Christ's passion and resurrection and compiled a collection of his sayings (known to the scholars as 'Q', which is short for the German *Quelle* – 'source').

Next, the evangelists were in a position to know the facts

about Jesus. St Mark moved, as we have seen, in the best apostolic circles where, if anywhere, the truth about Jesus was to be known. From his 'epistle dedicatory' (Luke 1.1-4) it is clear that St Luke knew a tradition derived from 'original eye-witnesses'. St John's Gospel rests back on ancient Palestinian tradition behind which probably stands the authority of the apostle John.

For a third consideration, the task of preserving what Jesus had said was facilitated by two factors: (1) Jesus had cast much of his teaching in the form of semitic poetry which – like our rhyme for remembering the months of the year – made it easier to remember; and (2) one third of his teaching recorded in the gospels consists of parables, those vivid short stories that have a way of sticking in the memory.

Fourth, the gospels – even St John's written in Ephesus – reflect the Palestinian scene in the first century AD: the towns and country places where this or that event occurred; the rulers in church and nation; the political and religious parties, ways of worship and ritual regulations. They mention the contemporary methods of farming, fishing, baking and housebuilding. Nor are we allowed to forget the weather and 'the wild life' of Palestine: sunshine and storm, flood and earthquake, the lilies of the field and the weeds among the wheat, wandering sheep and ravening wolves, the foxes and the sparrows.

Finally, through the gospels shines one fundamental portrait of their central figure, its authenticity forcing itself on any but the most prejudiced reader. It is that of one who is truly human – now happy, now sad; now pitiful, now stern; never blind to the evil in the human heart, yet ever gentle with the outcast and despised; swift to rebuke hypocrisy, yet ever believing that 'with God all things are possible', and no man or woman beyond his saving grace. This, on the one hand, and on the other, one who is more than mere man, one in whom there is something 'not of this world' which leaves the crowds in his presence 'amazed', 'awe-struck', 'astounded'; one who speaks with unheard-of authority, who possesses powers not given to other men, who is conscious of a unique relation to his heavenly Father and of being commissioned by him to do a work for men which none other can do.

A proper critical study of the gospels does not therefore lead to the conclusion that the original story concerned the life and death of an ordinary man, and that this story was later given a supernatural twist by the early Christians or Paul. The evangelists – St Mark no less than St John – believed they were witnesses to the life on earth of the Son of God. to his death on the cross for men's sins, and to his triumph over death. On this assumption they tell the story of Jesus in their differing way, and on this assumption it makes sense.

What then can the gospels tell us about the mission, message and person of Jesus?

First, using Mark's outline of events (which rests back on the apostles' preaching) and supplementing it from St John's special tradition, *we can reconstruct the general course of Jesus' ministry.*

All began after the Baptist's imprisonment when Jesus came into Galilee with the tremendous tidings of God's inbreaking kingdom and his call for repentance. Into their synagogues he went preaching and teaching until, when opposition to him grew, he resorted to the lakeside and his fame spread through the land. For those who had eyes to see, his healing miracles betokened the kingdom's presence. Then, choosing and training twelve men to be the nucleus of the new Israel, he sent them out to proclaim God's new order in word and deed and to gather his people. The climax came when in a desert place he fed five thousand men with the bread of the kingdom. It was the Galilean Lord's Supper.

Alas, by their reactions (John 6.15), the crowds showed they were dreaming of an all too human kingdom and

Messiah, so that Jesus now withdrew from Galilee, in order
that, in quiet, he might discover his Father's will for him.
By the time the little company had reached Caesarea
Philippi he knew. If the kingdom of God were to come
'with power', God's will for him as the Messiah meant
suffering and death. A week later he was transfigured on a
mountain top. Then came the march southwards to Judea
and a short ministry in Jerusalem (John 7.14-10.39) in
which he strove to alert the rulers of Jewry and the common
people to the great crisis now upon them, until, with
antagonism to him mounting, he retired briefly across the
Jordan (John 10.40-11.54), only to return to Jerusalem as
the Passover approached.

The rest is familiar: the Palm Sunday entry, the
cleansing of the temple, the priests' plot and the betrayal,
the Last Supper, the arrest in Gethsemane, the trial and
condemnation, and, finally, crucifixion, death and burial.
With his disciples gone into hiding, the mission of Jesus
seemed to have gone out in débâcle and death ...

Deo aliter visum. On the first day of the week three
women found the tomb empty, the crucified Messiah
appeared from heaven to his followers, the kingdom of God
had begun to 'come with power', the world-mission of his
apostles was about to begin.

Next, *the gospels provide us with a reliable account of
Jesus' teaching.* All is marked by his own highly individual
style – the swift surprises of thought, paradox, humour and
hyperbole, and his own daring and complete faith in his
heavenly Father. Jesus, we gather, liked to group his
teaching in threes ('Ask ... seek ... knock' etc.). He had a
way of prefacing a momentous saying with his own unique
'Amen I tell you' (a formula instinct with divine authority).
He had also a predilection for asking questions in order
to make the person addressed give his mind to the subject
and reach his own conclusion (e.g. 'Which of these three
proved neighbour to him who fell among the thieves?').

Here it is impossible to dwell at length on the content

of his religious and moral teaching. Its main burden was the dawning of that kingdom in which the king was an almighty Father and which he knew to be actualized in his own ministry. In the Sermon on the Mount (Matt. 5-7) he tells his disciples what kind of people God delights in, the goodness he demands, the worship he rewards, the service he requires, the faith to which he summons, the way he would have them treat other people. For the rest, from his recorded words we may learn what he thought concerning his own place in God's saving ways for men, how he construed the purpose of his sacrificial death, and what he believed about the future of history and God's final consummation of his kingdom in glory.

Finally, *the gospels furnish us with a portrait of the real Jesus.*

'The living eyes of a man', it has been said, 'look at us out of the gospels.' Now, if he is indeed, as we believe, the man in whom God came supremely into history, it is important to know what kind of man he was.

Jesus was neither legalist nor ascetic. Courage, humour and irony were his. He sympathized with women, as he had also a ready compassion for 'the underdog'. Human hearts he read unerringly; he could quicken in men new faith and hope, as he could make God real and near to them. Though ever gentle with guilt-ridden sinners, he could blaze out in indignation at wrong-doing. Above all, with a deep humility before God he conjoined a unique claim to divine authority, an awareness of unshared sonship to his Father above, and a conviction that he was God's 'apostle' to men in a decisive hour of history and that men's destinies hung upon their acceptance or rejection of himself.

Such is the person who dominates the gospels. Across nineteen centuries the lineaments of his character still shine clear.

We started from the question, Can we trust the gospels for the things that really matter for Christian faith? When we have made due allowance for some accretions which arose in the transmission of the gospel tradition and the adaptations which the apostles had to make when they applied, for example, Christ's teaching and parables to the new situation of the young churches, the answer to our question must be in the affirmative. After all sane and sensible criticism has had its say, we are left with three precious things: a trustworthy outline of that mission which changed the course of history, a reliable record of Christ's teaching, and an authentic portrait of the man himself. What more do Christians need today?

Nineteen centuries ago, St Matthew tells us, wise men came to Jesus. They still do.

PART TWO

6

The Kingdom of the Father

If one were asked to sum up in a single phrase the meaning of Jesus' mission and message, it would be hard to better T. W. Manson's five-word answer: 'the Kingdom of my Father'.[1] In the thought of the kingdom of his Father Jesus lived and worked and died. He believed that this kingdom which had been *initiated* in his ministry, would be *effectuated* by his own death and resurrection and would be *consummated* in glory when it pleased God to wind up the scroll of history.

But this is to anticipate conclusions. Let us begin at the beginning with the question, What is the kingdom of God?

Modern men have had their own way of interpreting the phrase. Some have taken it as the biblical equivalent of the doctrine of evolution, on the principle of—

> Some call it evolution,
> And others call it God.

Christian social reformers have construed it as some sort of earthly Utopia to be built by men on the teaching of Jesus. And some Roman Catholic scholars, following St Augustine, have equated the kingdom with the church. None of these answers is satisfactory.

The kingdom of God (*basileia tou theou*) means the kingly rule or reign of God; and if we are to understand it, we must think of it not territorially or statically but *dynamically*. It means the living God acting in his royal power, God visiting and redeeming his people. We may

define it as the sovereign activity of God in saving men
from sin and evil and the new order of things thus
established.

Now the kingdom of God, so understood, was for the
Jews *the* great hope of the future. It was another name for
the Messianic Age, for it connoted the whole salvation of
God, the event in which the whole long travail of history
would find its final meaning and God would complete his
saving purpose for the world.

It was with the proclamation that this kingdom was now
'upon them' that Jesus opened his mission to his countrymen. 'The time has come', he said, 'the kingdom of God
is upon you; repent and believe the gospel' (Mark 1.15).
The *eschaton*, or end event, for which they had been long
praying, was now breaking into history. This is what
scholars nowadays call 'inaugurated eschatology'; and if we
study the words and works of Jesus, we shall find ample
evidence to justify the phrase.

First, we come on sayings of Jesus which say explicitly
that the kingdom is a dawning reality. 'If I by the finger of
God cast out devils, then the kingdom of God has come
upon you.' (Luke 11.20, Q). 'The law and the prophets
were until John; since then the good news of the kingdom
of God is preached' (Luke 16.16, Q. In Matthew's version
the verb is *biazetai* 'exercises its force'). 'The kingdom of
God is in your midst' (Luke 17.21).

Next, we have sayings of Jesus which declare that the
ancient prophecies of the Day of the Lord are coming
true. Thus, 'blessed are the eyes which see what you see.
For I tell you that many prophets and kings desired to
see what you see, and did not see it, and to hear what you
hear, and did not hear it' (Luke 10.23f., Q).

Third, Jesus' 'mighty works' are, as he told John the
Baptist, signs of the presence and power of the kingdom.
'Go and tell John', he said to his messengers, 'what you have
seen and heard. The blind are receiving their sight, the
lame walking, the lepers are being cleansed, the dead are

being raised up, and the poor are having the good news preached to them' (Luke 7.22, Q).

Finally, Jesus' parables, one after another – the Sower, the Seed growing Secretly, the Leaven, the Seine Net, the Great Supper – all imply the reign of God as a dawning reality. All of them, observe, compare the reign of God not to some inert, static thing, but to something in movement, or to somebody doing something, and each of them says, in its different way, 'God is now among you in his royal and redemptive power. Now is the day of salvation.'

To the corollaries and consequences of this we must now turn.

The first concerns the king in his dawning kingdom. When Middleton Murray[2] wrote, 'The secret of the Kingdom of God was that there was no King, only a Father', his paradox contained truth. *The king in Jesus' kingdom was a Father.* 'When you pray', he bade his disciples, 'say "Father ... thy Kingdom come"' (Luke 11.2). 'Have no fear', he told them, 'your Father has chosen to give you the Kingdom' (Luke 12.32, NEB).

Let us however clear our minds of the common misconception that Jesus came proclaiming in public, 'God is your Father and you are all brothers'. The knowledge of God's Fatherhood was not something he shouted from the housetops or even revealed in parables, except in hints – as in his peerless story about the father and his two sons.

The facts are these: (1) Jesus himself addressed God as *Abba* ('dear Father'), the Aramaic word Jewish children used at home in talking to their earthly fathers. Before Jesus, no God-fearing Jew had ever dared to apply this 'caritative' – this term of endearment – to holy God. Jesus first did so; and if there were no other evidence, this alone would testify to his sense of unique Sonship. (2) In Mark, the earliest gospel, Jesus speaks of God as Father only four times, and always to disciples. God's Fatherhood was therefore a secret he disclosed to his own chosen followers in private. And if we ask why, the answer is, because the experience of God as Father was the last reality – the deepest secret – of his own spiritual life, something not easily to be talked about to all and sundry. (3) So far from teaching God's universal fatherhood (as if we were all, naturally, sons of God) what Jesus taught was that men might *become* sons of God. But for this supreme privilege they must become debtors to himself. What he said was, 'No one knows the Father but the Son and those to whom the Son may choose to reveal him' (Matt. 11.27, Q, NEB), 'No one comes to the Father except by me' (John 14.6).

Only with the coming of the Holy Spirit did Jesus' secret become an *open* secret. Then the chief word in Jesus' esoteric vocabulary became the precious possession of all God's adopted sons; and Paul, writing to the Christians in Rome, was able to say: 'The Spirit you have received is not a spirit of slavery leading you back into a life of fear, but a Spirit that makes us sons, enabling us to cry "Abba! Father!"' (Rom. 8.14f., NEB).

The second corollary is ecclesiastical – *the kingdom of God involves the church.*

One of our stateliest hymns begins:

> The Church's one foundation
> Is Jesus Christ our Lord,
> She is his new creation,
> By water and the Word.

But in what sense is the church Jesus' 'new creation'?

As we have seen, Jesus proclaimed that the rule or reign of God had begun. But is God an *emigré* ruler, a sovereign without a sphere of sovereignty? What kind of king is he who has no subjects? In other words, as convex involves concave, the very idea of a rule of God implies a people living under the divine rule, a church.

Take a second point. Kingdom and Messiah are correlates, one implying the other, for the basic idea of the Messiah is that he is the bearer of God's rule to men.

Though Jesus' concept of his Messiahship was utterly different from the popular concept of the 'Coming One', it is clear from the way he thought about it that he envisioned a new community, a new people of God. For the key to his own conception of Messiahship lies in two Old Testament figures, the Son of man in Daniel and Isaiah's Servant of the Lord. Both these figures are *societary* figures, i.e. both imply the formation of a community.

Take a further step. Jesus often spoke of himself as a shepherd and of his disciples as a flock. Shepherds and flocks were of course a familiar part of the Palestinian scene; but in Jesus' usage we have more than simply pastoral imagery. In the Old Testament (e.g. Ezek. 34) and in Jewish literature (e.g. The Psalms of Solomon, ch. 17) 'Shepherd' is one of the Messiah's names, as the Messiah's task is the gathering of God's flock.

In view of this not surprisingly some of Jesus' parables – e.g. the Mustard Seed, the Drag Net, the Wheat and the Tares – have clearly in view the creation of a new community, a church.

All this might be called the theological theory of the matter. When we turn to the gospels, what we see is Jesus *translating the theory into fact.*

First: *Jesus called twelve men and taught them.* Twelve was the number of the tribes in the old 'people of God'. Clearly Jesus is creating a new Israel, and instructing it. In what? In the ways of the dawning kingdom.

Second: *Jesus sent the twelve out as heralds of the kingdom.* What was the purpose of their mission? Let us recall that the rule of God is dynamic – it creates a people wherever its power is felt. Jesus' purpose, then, in sending out his missioners was the ingathering of God's people; and there is evidence enough in the gospels that it did not fail.

Third: *When Jesus held the Last Supper, it was an act in the establishment of his church.* At that supper, by means of broken bread and outpoured wine, Jesus gave

his disciples a share in the 'new covenant' to be inaugurated
by his death. Long before, at Sinai, God had constituted
the Hebrews into a people of God by making a covenant
with them (Ex. 24). The 'new covenant', now prophetically
inaugurated in the upper room, implies the creation of
a new 'people of God'. On the night of the Last Supper
the twelve sat as the nucleus of the new Israel, that
community which sprang into effective life after the
resurrection and on the Day of Pentecost was empowered by
God's Spirit for its appointed task.

The third corollary is moral – *the kingdom of God involves
a new style of living.*

What we call the moral teaching of Jesus, best summarized in the Sermon on the Mount (Matt. 5-7), is Jesus'
design for living in the kingdom of God. It is as if he were
saying to his men, 'Since the kingdom has dawned and
you are in it, you must begin to live in the kingdom way.'

As we shall discuss the matter more fully in later chapters
(on the Sermon on the Mount and the Christian ethic),
it will suffice to make only two points here.

First, the ethic of Jesus is not a new code of laws on the
perfect keeping of which our salvation depends. If it were,
we should all be doomed to damnation, since none of us
in this life measures up to the heights to which Jesus calls
us. Rather is it an *ethic of grace* – man's grateful response
in living to the grace of the God who brings in his kingdom.

Second, the most distinctive element in this new style
of life is the commandment of love *(agape)*. Jesus interprets
the whole duty of man to his fellow-man in terms of the
verb 'to love' (Mark 12.28-34). By 'love' he does not mean
anything sentimental or erotic, neither does he mean that
we must resolve to 'like' other people. By 'loving' he means
'caring' – caring practically and selflessly, as the Good
Samaritan did, for all who meet us on life's road, caring
not merely for the decent and the deserving, but for all
who need our help, even enemies. This is the new 'law' of

the kingdom because the king in the kingdom is a Father who himself cares for the ungracious and the ungrateful.

The fourth corollary is christological – *the kingdom is centred in Christ.*

'If *I* by the finger of God cast out devils, then the kingdom of God has come upon you' (Luke 11.20, Q). Here speaks one who embodies or incarnates the kingdom. Where he is, there is the kingdom, and to be his disciple is to be in it. Furthermore, many of Jesus' parables are burdened not only with 'the secret of the kingdom' (Mark 4.11) but with his own secret, for, at bottom, these two secrets are one. As Marcion perceived long ago, 'in the gospel the kingdom of God is Christ himself'.

Why then is this equation not clearer in the gospel record? The answer lies in what is known as 'the messianic secret'. Because the title was fatally loaded with political overtones—

> They all were looking for a King,
> To slay their foes and lift them high—

Jesus refused to proclaim himself publicly as the Messiah he knew himself to be. Instead, he chose the cryptic title of the Son of man – 'cryptic', because in Aramaic it could mean simply 'man' with a small 'm', or it could denote a mysterious Messianic figure.

The source of the title is to be sought in the famous vision of Daniel 7.[4] After the rise and fall of four beasts symbolizing the despotic heads of four world-empires (we still talk of 'the Russian Bear' and 'the British Lion') there appears 'one like a son of man' who receives from the Almighty a universal and eternal kingdom, or sovereignty. A few verses later, we are told that 'the saints of the Most High' (i.e. the people of God) shall receive the kingdom and possess it for ever.

'Son of man ... a kingdom ... the saints of the Most High.' Translate Daniel's apocalyptic theology into Galilean terms, and it reads: 'God gives the kingdom to Jesus' (cf. Luke 22.39 'My Father appointed a kingdom for me'), and he as the Son of man gives it to his disciples as the new people of God.

On Jesus' lips then the title 'Son of man' carried a veiled claim to be the bearer of God's sovereignty to men and the head of the new Israel. But in the gospels the Son of man, so far from being a triumphant figure, is one who must suffer and die if there is to be any sovereignty for him and his. Why? Because God has willed that the Son of man must tread the path marked out for the Servant of the Lord (Isa. 53).

One thing more needs to be said. Think of God's new order as a kingdom, and its bearer may well call himself the Son of man. But, if the king in the kingdom is a Father, only one word will describe him who brings it to men – the word 'Son'. This is why Jesus speaks of God as 'my Father' and calls himself God's Son, or 'the Son' (Matt. 16.17; Mark 1.11; 12, 1-9; 13.32; Matt. 11.27, Q). A filial relation to the Father, unique in history, is the last secret of the Jesus of the gospels.

The fifth corollary is – *the kingdom involves a cross.* Jesus is both the herald of the kingdom (Mark 1.15) and the Servant Son of man (Mark 10.45). He thus poses in his own person the problem of the kingdom and the cross.

Since, as we have seen, the kingdom was initiated in his ministry, we may not say that Jesus died to bring in the kingdom. The cross must fall *within* the kingdom, be its focus and climax. As the end which crowns his earthly work, it is the Messiah's last and bitterest battle in God's campaign against the powers of evil. 'Now is the judgment of this world, now shall the prince of this world be cast out' (John 12.31).

Near his ministry's beginning Jesus had spoken of the dawning kingdom as a 'secret' granted to his disciples (Mark 4.11). At Caesarea Philippi and afterwards he told them that God's appointed destiny for the Son of man was suffering and death, using language strongly redolent of

Isa. 53. Moreover, he prophesied that at no distant time men would see the kingdom of God come 'with power' (*en dunamei*, Mark, 9.1). Significantly, it is the very phrase the earliest Christians used of the resurrection (Rom. 1.3f). We may therefore say that the cross was the condition not of the kingdom's coming but of its effectuation in power. Nor is this unsupported speculation. It is confirmed by Jesus' saying about the 'fire' he came to kindle on earth and the baptism of blood he must undergo if the 'fire' were to be lit (Luke 12.49f.).[5]

The *Te Deum* is right. It was when Jesus had 'overcome the sharpness of death' that he 'opened the kingdom to all believers'.

Initiated in his ministry, effectuated by the cross and the resurrection, the kingdom which Jesus proclaimed yet awaits consummation. We Christians 'live between the times' – the time when God visited and redeemed his people in Jesus Christ his Son, and the time when he shall complete his great and gracious purpose in the glories of another and better world.

What had our Lord to say about the future and the end-time? Some of his sayings about the future kingdom (e.g. Matt. 8.11, Q, and Mark 14.25) clearly refer to the heavenly world where God's rule does not come or go but is *eternally present*. Others refer to a coming of the kingdom or of the Son of man – for the two are not to be separated – *in history*. Thus Jesus predicts that the Son of man will rise from the dead 'after three days' (Mark 8.31, i.e. a short, indefinite time, as in Hos. 6.2), or he tells the High Priest, 'You will see the Son of man sitting at the right hand of power and coming with the clouds of heaven' (Mark 14.62), a prediction, as Dan. 7.13 shows, of his exaltation to the presence of God. Apparent defeat by men, he means, will be followed by God's swift vindication, as indeed it was.

What actually happened is history: the Easter triumph

over death, the coming of the promised Spirit, the rise of the apostolic church. This was the coming of Christ in history, and St John, who mostly interprets it in terms of the advent of the Spirit, was not wrong.

Yet, if there was to be a coming in history, there was also to be another *beyond history*. When Christina Rossetti sang:

> Heaven and earth will flee away
> When he comes to reign

she had good warrant in the words of Jesus. In Luke 17.26-30 (Q), Jesus declares that the Son of man will be 'revealed' at the end of the existing order. In Mark 13.24-26 he pictures the dissolution of the physical universe before the Son of man comes. In his parable of the Last Judgment (Matt. 25.31-46) he sets the 'glorious' coming of the Son of man in another world than this. These sayings point to a coming of our Lord beyond history. This is the consummation of the kingdom. What will it mean?

First, the 'finalizing' of the work which God took in hand when he sent his Son into the world to redeem it. D-Day will have become V-Day, and God will be all in all. This is the point at which time – and all in history well-pleasing to God – will be taken up into his eternity.

Second, the confrontation of mankind by God in Christ. Here our clue is Christ's first coming. God has already revealed himself in a man from whom we may learn what sort of person we shall have to deal with when the human race reaches its last frontier post:

> Then will he come, with meekness for his glory,
> God in a workman's jacket as before,
> Living again the eternal gospel story,
> Sweeping the shavings from his workshop floor.[6]

That the consummation of the kingdom will involve judgment – whatever form it takes – is the teaching of both Christ and his apostles. At that final 'sifting' (which is the basic meaning of judgment) the criteria will be men's response to such revelation of God and his truth as were available to them in their day and generation (Luke 11.31ff., Q), and the compassion they have shown to all needy folk whom Christ calls his 'brethren' (Matt. 25.31-46).

But, equally, the consummation will mean the perfect fruition of life in the eternal world of God, the wiping away of all tears, the triumph of Christ and his saints.... Then the promises of the Beatitudes will come fully true: the mourners will be comforted, the merciful will obtain mercy, the pure in heart will see God, and his faithful children will be for ever at home in their Father's house.

When will this consummation take place? We do not know, nor did the Son of God himself (Mark 13.32). It is a reserved secret in the breast of God. Nor is it the Christian's business to speculate on 'the day or the hour'. New Testament thought on the last things, at its deepest and best, always concentrates on what God has already done for men in Christ.[7] It does not say, How long will it be before the final whistle blows 'full time'. Rather it asks, 'Where ought I to be to receive the next pass?' What really matters is that the kick-off has already taken place, the game is on, and we have a captain to lead us to victory.

NOTES

1. *The Sayings of Jesus*, SCM Press 1949, p. 345.
2. *The Life of Jesus*, p. 37.
3. In Greek the 'I' is emphatic.
4. J. Jeremias, *New Testament Theology Vol. I*, SCM Press 1971, pp. 268ff.
5. Mark 9.1 does not refer to the end or parousia. It *implies* that from Jesus' viewpoint the coming of the kingdom with power is a future event, but what it *states* is that the time will come when some of the bystanders will look back on it as a past event. See G. B. Caird in *Biblical Studies: Essays in Honour of William Barclay*, ed. Johnston R. McKay and James F. Miller, Collins 1976, p. 74.
6. G. A. Studdert-Kennedy.
7. C. F. D. Moule, *The Birth of the New Testament*, A. & C. Black 1962, pp. 101f.

7

The Works of the Kingdom

When the son of E. V. Rieu, Editor of the Penguin Classics, heard that his father had begun to translate the gospels, he is reported to have said, 'It will be interesting to see what father makes of the gospels, and still more interesting to see what the gospels make of him'. So it proved. When the new translation appeared, E. V. Rieu, in his preface, confessed that his long task had 'changed' him. Now he was convinced that the gospels 'bore the seal of the Son of man and of God'. What was the chief impression which the ministry of Jesus had left upon his mind? A dynamic one. It was (he said) that of 'a strong wind sweeping through Palestine': 'one of power, tremendous power, utterly controlled'.[1]

'Power' is the literal meaning of *dynamis*, the usual word in the gospels for miracle, and normally translated 'mighty work'. Jesus saw his 'mighty works' as 'outgoings' of the divine *dynamis*, the power of the creator God whom he called 'Father' and for whom, he said, 'all things were possible' (Mark 10.27), the Father who ruled over his world in righteousness and love with utter constancy and infinite care.

Some people would like a story of Jesus without miracles because they imagine (mistakenly, as we shall see) that modern science has shown them to be impossible. But no account of the Jesus of history – the real Jesus – can have any claim to authenticity which does not find proper room for his dynamic deeds as well as his wonderful words.

There is another consideration. No careful student of the gospels can miss Jesus' clear conviction that his ministry was a supreme turning-point in human affairs, a historical crisis destined to inaugurate a new set of relations (the biblical word is 'covenant') between God and men.

Now if it is true, as C. S. Lewis says in his sparkling book on miracles,[2] that God does not shake them into nature at random as if from a pepper caster, that they come on the great occasions, are found at 'the great ganglions (or nerve-centres) of history', should we not expect Jesus' ministry to be marked by miracles which we may define as exceptional occurrences bringing with them an undeniable sense of the presence and power of God?

So in fact it proves. Miracles bulk large in the gospels. No gospel source lacks them – even the scholars' 'Q' which is a collection of Jesus' sayings. About one third of Mark, the earliest gospel, is concerned with miracles. Modern man, 'blinded by science' and attributing to it sometimes a quasi-omniscience which any reputable scientist would downrightly deny, is apt to rank the gospel miracles with the fairy tales of his childhood (e.g. about Santa Claus) – 'childish innocencies' no longer credible by the adult *homo sapiens* of today. But what he may not deny, if he seriously studies the matter, is that miracle belongs to the very stuff of the gospel. Part of its primary stratum, the miracles demand a place in any scientific reconstruction of Jesus' ministry.

Miracles then being no more separable from the gospel record than the water-mark from a sheet of note-paper, we have three questions before us calling for answers:

What place did the miracles have in Jesus' good news?
What were their characteristics?
How far are they credible today?

The burden of all Jesus' preaching was the kingdom of God, i.e. the sovereign activity of God in saving men from their sins, overcoming evil, and establishing his new order of grace. It was the very heart of his 'good news' that this new dispensation was no longer a shining hope on the far horizon but a dawning and blessed reality in his own ministry. For Jesus, his mighty works, or miracles, were tokens of that new era in which the power of God was at work through himself and his mission, meeting and defeating the devil and all his works, whether it was the demonic distortion of man's personality, or the assault of disease on his natural vigour, or the foretaste of death, 'the last enemy'. In short, the mighty works of Jesus were the *reign of God in action*, outgoings in power to sick and sinful men and women of that holy love which was central to the kingdom of his Father.

Miracle in the sense of 'prodigy' Jesus disesteemed, whether the request came from the devil, King Herod, or the Pharisees. No thaumaturge, he steadfastly refused to work 'wonders' in order to *compel* men into belief in himself. No such 'sign', i.e. legitimating proof of his own authority, he said, would be given (Mark 8.12; Luke 11.29f., Q).

Nonetheless, he regarded his 'works' as an integral part of his message. If by word and parable he proclaimed the kingdom's dawning and challenged his hearers, by repentance and faith, to accept his good news, his dynamic deeds were also signs, for those who had eyes to see, that the Almighty was now visiting his people in judgment and mercy. Charged by his opponents with using 'black magic', he replied, 'If I by the finger of God cast out demons, then the kingdom of God has come upon you' (Luke 11.20; Matt. 12.28, Q; for 'finger' Matthew has 'Spirit'). It is but the other side of the same coin to note that Jesus saw his mighty works as fulfilling the prophets' predictions about the Messianic Age. Thus, when John the Baptist sent messengers from his prison to enquire, 'Are you the Coming One (i.e. the Messiah)?' Jesus replied, in effect, 'You remember what Isaiah prophesied about blind men receiving their sight, deaf men hearing, lame men walking and dead men being raised to life? These things are happening here. Draw your own conclusions. But happy is the man who is repelled by nothing in me' (Luke 7.18-23; Matt. 11.2-6, Q). It is as if he were saying, 'I am the Messiah, but hardly the kind you, John, were expecting'.

To sum up. 'The works of Christ' (Matt. 11.2) were the signs of the inbreaking rule of God, and 'divinely happy' (*makarios*) were those who could see them so and discern in their doer God's apostle to men.[3]

If Jesus' miracles were tokens of the dawning reign of God, what were their characteristics?

Surveying them first from the human angle, note the strong stress Jesus lays on the need for *faith*. Confidence in his God-given power to heal is a pre-condition of his power to do so – the sphere wherein faith comes to fruition. Where such faith is lacking, as in his native Nazareth (Mark 6.5), this power is ineffectual. Where it is present, as Jesus tells the father of the epileptic boy (with his, 'I have faith, help me where faith falls short' (Mark 9.23, NEB)), 'all things are possible'. So he says to Jairus when the professional mourners are already lamenting his daughter's death, 'Fear not; only have faith' (Mark 5.36).

Of a piece with this is the demand which Jesus often makes for the patient's co-operation. 'Have you the will to health?' he asks the cripple at the Pool of Bethesda (John 5.6). Elsewhere his commands to the sick, e.g. 'Take up your bed and walk' (Mark 2.11), are invitations to co-operate in the cure. A like faith Jesus found also in the sheer pertinacity of people who sought his help for themselves or those whom they represented. One thinks of blind Bartimaeus who refused to be discouraged by the bystanders (Mark 10.46-52), or the paralytic's four friends who took down a bit of the roof in order to get him into Jesus' presence (Mark 2.1-5). This faith is no mere pale, passive believing: it is the importunate grasping after God's help present in Jesus.

Consonant with all this is the emphasis which Jesus sets on prayer, which is really faith in action. Compare Mark 9.20f. and 11.24. We moderns, half-hypnotized by the apparently 'steel-and-concrete' order of nature, wonder what we may pray for. Jesus had no such hesitations about the power of prayer.

Yet faith and prayer are but one half – the human half – of the secret of Jesus' miracles. What of the divine side? 'By the finger (or Spirit) of God' is Jesus' answer. His mighty works are evidence of God's Spirit working through himself.

At his baptism Jesus had known himself to be 'anointed with the Spirit', that is, equipped with divine power. Except on this assumption, his 'temptations' in the wilderness are unreal. To the same effect are his words in the Nazareth synagogue, 'The Spirit of the Lord God is upon me' (Luke 4.16-21). He regards not only his preaching of the 'good news to the poor' but also his conquests of disease and the devil as inspired by the puissant Spirit of God. His own 'acts of power' reveal the energizing of God's Spirit through himself for the saving of sick and sinful men and women. 'The Father who dwells in me does his works', is how he puts it in John's Gospel (John 14.10).

'I think', wrote David S. Cairns, author of one of the finest books on the miracles, 'I think the Gospel view of the miracles is, quite plainly, that they are the work of His [Jesus'] own faith in God, and of the Divine Spirit in answer to the appeal of His faith.'[4]

So, last, to the question of the credibility of the miracles. Two preliminary points may be made. First, we must always be satisfied that any particular narrative is really a miracle story and that the historical evidence for it is good. Moreover, doubt concerning any alleged miracle does not of course discredit the lot.

Second, Jesus' contemporaries had not our modern understanding of 'secondary causes' and sought a supernatural explanation for any event that baffled their comprehension, like Daniel Defoe's pious lady who, on seeing a bottle of ripe beer explode and fly in froth to the ceiling, exclaimed 'O the wonders of Omnipotent Power!' In the case of some apparently 'miraculous' events recorded in the gospels no such 'supernatural' explanation may be necessary.

With these two provisos, let us now essay an answer to the main question.

No Christian with a respect for his intellectual integrity need doubt that Jesus restored sight to the blind, helped deaf men to hear again, enabled lame men to walk, cleansed lepers, cured those thought to be possessed by evil spirits, and brought back to life those apparently dead. For these miracles the historical evidence is excellent, and in support we may point to the advances made in psychosomatic medicine, the recognition of the potent part played by mind in the cause and cure of disease, and the evidence of what has been called 'the forgotten talent', faith-healing.

True, our doctors, psychiatrists and faith-healers cannot match the speed of Jesus' recorded cures, and his ability to heal at a distance poses problems for some. But if – to put it at its lowest – we remember the extraordinary personality of Jesus, we shall wisely refuse to say that we will only accept those miracles which we, with our present skills and knowledge, can effect. And the secret of his 'telepathic' healings – the officer's son and the Syro-Phoenician woman's daughter – is surely to be sought in the person of Jesus and the divine answers to the appeal of his faith.

But did Jesus really still a storm, feed five thousand people with five loaves and two fishes, walk on the Lake of Galilee, and fatally curse a fig-tree which had leaves but no fruit on it in early April?

Here a wise biblical criticism can help. There is much in the gospel record to suggest that the feeding of the multitude was not a miracle but a sacrament – what has been called 'the Galilean Lord's Supper'.[5] It has often been noted that St John's account of the walking on the water need not be miraculous at all, since the crucial phrase in Greek *epi tes thalasses* would naturally mean, as it in fact does in John 21.1, *'by the sea'*. The point of the story is Jesus' unexpected appearance to his disciples in the hour of their fear and danger.[6] Remembering Jesus' parable of the Barren Fig-tree (Luke 13.6-9), we may regard the so-called 'cursing' as an acted parable of the divine judgment he knew to overhang Israel – like, in fact, the prophetic *ōth* of Jeremiah in the Old Testament (Jer. 19.1-13). Finally, why should not the stilling of the storm be taken as a miracle of divine providence? 'Jesus trusted in God, and his trust was not deceived.'[7]

The other fact bearing on this question of credibility is the remarkable change that has come over our understanding of the universe. Not so long ago men supposed that because science had revealed it to be a cast-iron system of natural law, miracles, being violations of it, were impossible. (The trouble started when Liberal Protestants like Ernest Renan and Matthew Arnold turned the *working hypotheses* of natural science into *theological dogmas*.) We know now that the so-called 'laws of nature' are merely convenient summaries of existing knowledge, constantly needing to be revised. But, more than this, 'matter' which we used to regard as 'hard fact' is now disclosed to be a very storehouse of wonders, and he would be a very bold man indeed who could pronounce what is, or what is not, possible. Nowadays, whatever the science of the popular press may say, all true men of science recognize that man's intelligence is a very limited instrument, and that the corpus of their scientific knowledge is like a pebble on the vast shore.

Christians cannot therefore surrender the concept of miracle at the sceptic's bidding. On the contrary, the very triumphs of our modern scientists reveal to those who take the Christian view a God infinitely greater than even the sublime fortieth chapter of Isaiah depicts. If ingenious modern man can so cleverly harness what we call nature to his chosen ends, Christians are entitled to say, How much more shall not the creator, who is our heavenly Father, be able to manipulate his creation to his own gracious purposes! When he elects to do so, he does not infringe the laws of nature. Rather, miracle is 'the occasion when the Supreme Artist, whose command of brush and medium is complete, does with an easy turn of the wrist what the earnest apprentice vainly strives to do with knotted brow and straining fingers'.[8]

The final fact – and for Christians the decisive one – is the *person of Christ*, the man whom we have good reason for believing God raised from the dead.

If Jesus was, as he undoubtedly claimed to be, the only Son of God, in whom the divine Spirit was incarnate and active, and if his ministry was nothing less than God invading history to defeat the powers of evil that had lodged not only in human beings but in the created world, why should it be thought incredible that to such a person, united in fellowship with nature's creator, the natural world would prove responsive in quite new and unparalleled ways?

Without miracle there can be no Christianity, but merely 'religion', a religion in which, as Carlyle once petulantly complained to Froude, 'God does nothing' and therefore no miracle. Such a God is not the living God of the Bible whose workshop is history. Most certainly he is not the God and Father of our Lord Jesus Christ, concerning whom he said, 'My Father is working still, and I am working' (John 5.17). The God whom Christians worship is the God who delivered Israel at the Red Sea and took Jesus out of the. tomb, raising him to high heaven. For such a God, the divine art of miracle is not the art of breaching nature's laws or of suspending the regular pattern of events. His is the art of feeding new and extraordinary happenings into that history of which he is Lord, of interposing sovereignly in that order of nature which is his creation.

In a word, he is the God both of nature and of grace, whose mighty acts are to be seen not only in the returning snowdrops and in the annual miracle of Spring, but also in 'the great ganglions of history', the God who is even now shaping its course, in ways past human fathoming, to that blessed pattern and end revealed to us Christians, once for all, in the life, death and resurrection of Jesus Christ his Son.

NOTES

1. *The Four Gospels*, Penguin Books 1952, pp. xxxf.
2. C. S. Lewis, *Miracles*, Fontana 1960, p. 171.
3. In John's Gospel Jesus is called 'the-sent-of-God' 44 times.
4. *David Cairns, An Autobiography*, SCM Press 1950, p. 193.
5. The phrases describing Jesus' actions recall the Last Supper. Had it been a miracle, Jesus would have been acting like a 'Bread Messiah' – the very role he had repudiated in the wilderness; and the disciples' later worry about bread (Mark 8.16) would make no sense. In John's independent account of the feeding, stress is laid on its sacramental significance: 'I am the bread of life' etc.
6. C. H. Dodd, *Historical Tradition in the Fourth Gospel*, Cambridge University Press 1963, p. 198.
7. Vincent Taylor, *The Gospel According to Mark*, Macmillan 1952, p. 273.
8. A. C. Craig, *Preaching in a Scientific Age*, p. 73.

8

Repentance and Faith

'The time has come; the kingdom of God is upon you; repent and believe' (Mark 1.15, NEB).

With this proclamation Jesus began his ministry. What he meant by the kingdom of God we have considered. But what did he mean by 'repent and believe' which was the *sine qua non* of entry into it?

Once, when puzzled by the Vulgate's rendering of the Greek for 'repent' (*metanoeite*) by 'do penance', Martin Luther sought an answer from his friend Melanchthon, an expert in Greek. *Metanoeite*, he was told, means 'change your mind'. So, T. R. Glover observed that Luther learnt the true meaning of 'repentance' – that it means 're-thinking' – and grasped a new idea of God.[1]

But did Melanchthon and Glover, good 'Grecians' both, get it right? Was Jesus merely calling on his countrymen to change their ideas of God?

Expertise in classical Greek does not, by itself, make you always a sound interpreter of New Testament Greek, for the simple reason that all the New Testament writers (save Luke) were Jews, and their Greek words were often stained with Hebrew meanings. *Metanoia*, 'repentance', is one such. Nowadays our scholars agree that for its true meaning we must consult the Hebrew prophets and their use of the verb *shubh* which signifies 'turn' or 'return':

> Come let us to the Lord our God
> With contrite hearts return (Hos. 6.1).[2]

The basic idea here is that of rebellious subjects coming back to serve God their rightful king. (Note: the Greek idea of 'repentance' limits the meaning to an intellectual change, as it lacks the Godward reference of repentance in the Bible.) What Jesus meant by 'repentance' was a right-about-turn of the whole person, a re-orientation of one's whole life: 'Turn away from your sins and back to God.'

Our Lord's best picture of repentance is to be found in his parable about the Prodigal Son. 'It was not repentance', Mrs William Booth is reported as saying, 'when the prodigal grew hungry, or even when he said, "I will arise and go to my father". You see repentance where it is said, "And he *arose and went* to his father".' How right she was!

By the evidence of the gospels both Jesus and his fore-runner John the Baptist said, 'Repent!' But did they mean the same thing? On the contrary, John said, 'Repent, for the day of wrath is near' (Matt. 3.1ff.). Jesus said, 'Repent, for the reign of God is here'. That is to say, in the message of Jesus *repentance and grace have changed places*. For John, as for the Old Testament prophets and the Pharisees, repentance was the first and necessary condition of being saved on the coming day of divine judgment. For Jesus, the hour of God's great grace has already struck, and his summons means, 'Lay hold upon it now, by turning back to God'. In other words, true Christian repentance springs from 'prevenient grace' – from the knowledge that God is now inaugurating a new era which brings with it a new covenant of forgiveness, deliverance from sin, and the outpouring of the Holy Spirit.

But Jesus said 'Repent *and believe*'. In his view, repentance and faith are inseparably connected. If we study the stories of Mary of Magdala, the woman who was a sinner, and the little superintendent of taxes in Jericho, we see that their encounter with Christ produced both these things in their hearts. And both are God's gifts, not men's achievements. To awaken to repentance is, in the same act, to awaken to saving faith. For, as repentance means turning away from sin, so faith means turning to God. It is no wonder therefore that the earliest apostolic preaching always contained a call to repentance, for without it true faith is impossible.

But in Jesus' teaching not only have repentance and grace changed places, but repentance has become not a call to lament but to *rejoice*.

What a joyless crowd many of the Pharisees in Jesus' day seem to have been! They grumbled because he sat down at table with notorious sinners. They complained that his disciples behaved like men at a wedding instead of wearing the grave looks of men in deadly earnest about their religion. They dismissed Jesus as a 'bon viveur' and a glutton.

How differently Jesus conceived the whole business of penitence and fasting! 'Fast if you will', he told his disciples, 'but do it in secret. Never look gloomy. Rather wash your face, anoint your head, and be like men on their way to a party' (Matt. 6.16-18). Glad gratitude for God's goodness should be the mood of a true repentance, as its keynote should be that of the father's welcome to his returning prodigal: 'How could we help celebrating this happy day? Your brother here was dead and has come back to life, was lost and is found' (Luke 15.32, NEB).

But if the Pharisees apparently believe that holy things are by no means to be enjoyed – as some of our Puritan forefathers did – have we modern Christians learned the secret of how to be both 'good and gay'?

Nowadays 'repentance' is a word that has gone right out of fashion. It conjures up for many the 'awful warnings' of old-time preachers and outmoded doctrines of 'total depravity' and a God who 'sends one to heaven and ten to hell, all for his glory'.[3] So we erase the word from our working vocabulary and find ourselves – happier? No, more depressed than ever. Why?

In one of his essays Dr Nathaniel Micklem[4] traces this widespread depression among modern Christians to the loss of the doctrines of original sin and evangelical grace. When, he says, recognizing that you are a hell-deserving sinner – and are not afraid to admit it – and when you believe in him who (great and glad paradox) 'justifies the ungodly', it is much more natural to think of grace and be happy than to think of sin and be depressed.

John Ruskin was of the same opinion.[5] 'You hear much nowadays of conversion', he wrote, 'but people always seem to think they have got to be made wretched by conversion, to be converted to long faces. No, friends, you have got to be converted to short ones – to repent into delight and delightsomeness.'

And 'repent into delight and delightsomeness' many modern Christians should, would they but really believe what they profess to believe – believe that 'this is our Father's world' and that he has come into it to redeem it, that by the cross and resurrection his Son Jesus Christ has triumphed over sin and death and now lives and reigns in highest heaven, and that he is still with us through his *alter ego*, the Holy Spirit – that Spirit who, the apostles tell us, is the pledge and promise of all those blessed things in store for his 'saints' when it shall please God to consummate his kingdom in glory.

'Look to him, and be radiant', said the psalmist (Ps. 34.5, RSV) centuries before a babe was born in Bethlehem. But have not we Christians who live in the light of God's supreme revelation of himself in Christ much better reason for so doing?

NOTES

1. *The Jesus of History*, SCM Press 1917 edition, p. 231.
2. Scottish Paraphrases, *Church Hymnary* (revised) 30.
3. Robert Burns, 'Holy Willie's Prayer'.
4. Micklem, *No More Apologies*, p. 120.
5. John Ruskin, *The Crown of Wild Olive*.

9

The Sermon on the Mount

Few would deny that the Sermon on the Mount (Matt. 5-7; cf. Luke 6.20-49) is the greatest moral manifesto in history. Yet how differently men have construed it! For Tolstoy, it was a new law, superseding the law of Moses, to be interpreted quite literally, and of universal application. For Schweitzer, it was Jesus' 'ethic for the interval' – that brief interval between his ministry and a cataclysmic end of the world which never came. Very different is the view of writers in the popular press when it turns 'religious'. They evidently suppose it to be 'plain sailing' – straightforward rules for living which, could they but be written into the statute-books of the nations, would usher in heaven on earth. It is then that others arise to query this 'plain sailing' and to ask: Is the Sermon indeed a morality for all men? So the debate goes on. Some, like Gandhi, would tell us that the Sermon contains the essence of the gospel, only to provoke an emphatic protest from others that the gospel is something God has *done* for men, and not simply something he *demands* of them. What is the real truth?

For a start, let us be clear what the Sermon is and what it contains. The Sermon, which gathers together into one splendid whole teaching which Jesus gave his disciples on various occasions, has seven main themes:

    (1) The kind of people God calls divinely happy (5.3-16)

    (2) The goodness he demands (5.17-48)

    (3) The worship he rewards (6.1-18)

    (4) The service he requires (6.19-24)

    (5) The faith to which he summons (6.25-34)

(6) The way he would have us treat others (7.1-12)

(7) Profession must issue in practice (7.13-28).

Three questions arise: (1) What is the Sermon's place in the New Testament's good news? (2) Is it teaching for the disciples of Jesus, or for all men? (3) Is it a new law, replacing that of Moses?

We cannot begin to understand the Sermon until we set it against the background of the gospel Jesus came preaching: 'The kingdom of God is upon you. Repent and believe' (Mark 1.15). The burden of all Jesus' words and works was the announcement that the reign of God had begun. This is the *prius* and presupposition of all that he says in the Sermon. The Sermon in fact sketches the way of life for all those who, by repentance and faith, have responded to the good news of God's forgiving grace which the dawning of his rule brings with it.

If Jesus says, 'You must forgive others', it is because they have already received the divine assurance, 'Your sins are forgiven'. If he bids his hearers live as 'sons of God', it is because, through him, they know themselves to be God's adopted sons. If he commands them to 'love their enemies', behind the command lies the dynamic of the boundless grace of God who is 'kind to the unthankful and the evil'. 'There must be no limits to your goodness', he tells them, 'as your heavenly Father's goodness knows no bounds' (Matt. 5.48, NEB). It is a case of 'Freely you have received. Therefore freely give'. In a word, the ethic of the Sermon is *an ethic of grace*.

We may now essay answers to our three questions:

First, the Sermon is not the gospel itself but its *corollary for living*. The good news tells of something God has *done* – that in Christ he has come into the world to redeem it. But this good news carries with it a consequence for conduct. Those who by following Jesus are 'in the kingdom' must live in 'the kingdom way'. This way the Sermon outlines.

From this it follows that the Sermon is essentially *disciple-teaching*. It is meant for the 'men of the kingdom', not primarily for all and sundry. It is for all who confess Jesus as Master and Lord.

But did Jesus intend the Sermon as a kind of new law of Moses on the perfect keeping of which men's salvation would depend? If this had in fact been his intention, he who invited men weighed down by the law's burdens, to 'come to him', 'take his yoke upon them', and 'find relief' (Matt. 11.28ff.), would have been laying on his disciples heavier loads than ever the Scribes and Pharisees laid on theirs (Matt. 23.4). This is incredible. Jesus was no such legislator. What he gave his followers in the Sermon was principles of action to govern their lives in the new order of God's grace. The Sermon is not a new code of laws but a pattern for living. It is a compass, not an ordnance map. It provides direction, not directions.

But 'direction' for actual living, or a counsel of perfection? – this is the question, and we believe the right answer to it is, 'both'.

'You can receive a sacrament and you can find salvation', says one of Rose Macaulay's characters, 'but you can't live the Sermon on the Mount.' Well, evidently even Jesus' first disciples found it hard to live 'the kingdom way'. 'Why do you keep calling me "Lord, Lord"', he said, 'and never do what I tell you?' (Luke 6.46, NEB). Yet that he meant his teaching to be translated into action is proved by the parable of the Two Builders at the Sermon's end. In it he says in effect, 'Either you act my way, which is God's way, or you court disaster'.

Today many still take the view that 'you can't live the Sermon on the Mount'. They pronounce its teaching impossibly idealistic and, in evidence, appeal to what Jesus says about 'turning the other cheek' and 'loving enemies'. What, they ask, would have happened to us in

74

1939 if we had meekly 'turned the other cheek' to Hitler and tried to 'love' his Nazis?

This question does not arise in Matt. 5.38-42, where Jesus is talking to his disciples about personal relations. He is not telling them never to resist evil. His word to them is: 'Do not set yourself against the man who wrongs you' (Matt. 5.39, NEB). What he is inculcating is the principle of overcoming evil with good, and he drives his point home with four picturesque – and hyperbolic – illustrations. The first is an assault; the second, a suit at law; the third, an official demand; and the fourth, a request for help.

The phrase about 'turning the other cheek' has hidden humour in it. 'If a man smites you on the right cheek' he says – a pause while each disciple thought furiously about what was to be done; but Jesus' completion of his sentence must have taken their breaths away, 'Well, you have another one!'

As for the second illustration, a man who presented his opponent with both his 'shirt' and 'coat' would find himself in a state of near nudity – evidence enough that this hyperbole was meant to illustrate a principle.

In the third illustration we are to picture a Roman soldier 'commandeering' a passing Jew with, 'Here shoulder my baggage, and get moving!' 'When this happens and you have done the mile he demanded', says Jesus, 'disarm him by carrying his bag another mile.' The principle is that of countering harshness with kindness.

'Give to him who begs from you', reads, *prima facie*, like a command to indiscriminate almsgiving, and everybody knows to what evils this can lead. Once again, however, it is a principle – that of generous reaction to human need – which is being enforced.

Take then these sayings of Jesus *au pied de la lettre* and you miss their real meaning. A literal obedience to them (such as Tolstoy desired) would merely result in violence, robbery and anarchy.

75

Even so, it may be asked, does this teaching validate itself in actual practice? It does. There are cases and situations without number where Jesus' principle does justify itself in practice, and good people do in fact carry it out. To stifle an angry reaction to a personal insult, to respond to harshness with kindness, to go the second mile, to be open-handed to the needy, is not this 'the kingdom way' and do not such actions wonderfully sweeten human relations in a hard and selfish world?

Consider next Jesus' teaching about 'loving enemies' (Matt. 5.43-48). Does this mean that Christians should regard benignly organizations like the IRA Provisionals who inflict suffering and death on innocent people? Most certainly it does not. Once again, it is not attitudes to enemies of the state, but personal relations, which are in view. Moreover, 'love' is not synonymous with 'like'. There are people, as Jesus well knew, whom we do not naturally 'take to' or 'like'. How, for instance, can we 'like' people who lead our children astray or break up our marriage? When Jesus tells his followers to 'love their enemies', he does not mean to 'love' them as they do their wives and children. No, but he does command them to 'copy God' who sends his sun and rain on good and bad alike. Whether we 'like' certain people or not, we are to 'care' for them – treat them with persistent and practical good-will, simply because such 'caring' is God's way.

We have been arguing that Christ's teaching about 'turning the other cheek' and 'loving enemies' is not so 'impossible', as many people think. Yet, if some still maintain that the Sermon's teaching is 'beyond them', let us remember that he who called on men to put his teaching into practice, also described it as a counsel of perfection. 'You therefore must be perfect', he said, 'as your heavenly Father is perfect' (Matt. 5.48). Was not our Lord right in so saying? Is not this what a true Christian ethic should ever be?

The Sermon on the Mount

> A man's reach should exceed his grasp.
> Or what's a heaven for?

No man or woman, however saintly, ever measures up the Sermon's standards. We judge ourselves by them and know we are sinners who come far short of the glory of God. Yet if none ever attains the heights set before us in the Sermon, this but exemplifies the tension between the ideal and the actual which must always, in this world, be our lot. We who are citizens of a 'commonwealth' which is in heaven (Phil. 3.20), have nonetheless to live out our lives in a world where evil and temptations beset us every way. Yet though the moral ideal of the Sermon must ever remain beyond our 'grasp', we are yet called, with divine help, day by day to keep on striving towards it.

In spite of Jeremiah, St Paul[1] and Robert Browning, we are not mere clay in the great potter's hand. In Christ, we are children of an almighty Father. Even so, may we not fitly make our own the prayer of Rabbi ben Ezra:

> So take and use Thy work!
> Amend what flaws may lurk!
> What strain o' the stuff, what warpings past the aim!
> My times be in His hand!
> Perfect the cup as planned!
> Let age approve of youth, and death complete the same![2]

NOTES

1. Jeremiah 18.1-10 (the parable of the potter), Rom. 9.20ff. (A man is not a pot. He will say, Why did you make me so?)
2. Robert Browning, 'Rabbi ben Ezra'.

77

10

The Books Jesus Read

Robert Flint, once Professor of Divinity in Edinburgh
University, used to tell his students that, if they would
preach effectively, they must study both nature and human
nature. First-hand study of both was best. But, he added,
if you cannot conveniently study nature in this way, read
Wordsworth; and if you cannot easily study human nature
thus, read Shakespeare.

Sage counsel – so far as it goes. Yet Flint's prescription
for study, as reported by one of his students, contains one
notable omission. No student of the gospels can fail to note
that the greatest preacher of all read not in two books but
in three – the Book of Nature, the Book of Human Nature
and the Book of the People of God.

Of Jesus' reading in the 'open volume' of nature the
gospels contain examples in plenty. None better than he
exemplifies Pascal's saying: 'They pay great honour to
Nature who show her able to discourse on all things, even
theology.' (So thought also Nancy Mitford in our day when
Raymond Mortimer tried to turn her into an agnostic.
'How', she replied tartly, 'How can you say we know
literally nothing of Somebody among whose works we
live?')

To nature Jesus goes continually for illustrations of the
will and ways of God. Best-known perhaps is his, 'Consider
the lilies of the field, how they grow'. For Jesus, these
scarlet anemones which, because they grew so abundantly,

the women used to fuel their kitchen stoves, were finer far than Solomon in all his glory. 'Today they are,' he said, 'and tomorrow they are not.' It is an old motif, this of the transience of life as seen in the fading flower, but Jesus gives it a new turn. His lesson is not, 'These perish, and so must we'. It is: 'God lavishes infinite pains on these, brief though their life is. How much more does he care for you his children!'

In the sunshine and the rain, falling on good and bad alike, he finds evidence of the grace of God. In the mystery of unfolding buds – first the green shoot, then the spike of corn, and then the full grain in the ear – he would have impatient men find an analogy of how the new divine force released in the world – the kingdom of God – grows irresistibly, inevitably, from seed-time to harvest. A man sowing seed on a neighbouring hill-side evokes from him a parable about the almighty sower and his harvest which, in spite of failures, exceeds all expectation. A shepherd's concern for a lost sheep furnishes him with a figure for his own work as the divine shepherd who goes seeking out and saving God's lost children. A hen with her chickens under her wings serves him as simile of how often he had sought – alas, in vain – to gather God's ancient people into his Father's kingdom. Thus:

> Christ talked of grass and wind and rain,
> And figtrees and fair weather,
> And made it his delight to bring
> Heaven and earth together,[1]

as nature's book provided him with—

> Pictures from the page of life,
> Teaching by parable.[2]

What did nature say to him about 'the high and holy one who inhabits eternity'? To Old Testament psalmist and prophet (e.g. Ps. 19 and Isa. 40) nature had spoken of the might and majesty of God. So too it did to Christ. 'Lord of heaven and earth', he names God (Matt. 11.25), but in the word he prefixes to it, we find the deep difference between the Old Testament and the New. It is the word 'Father'. At the inmost heart of reality Jesus found one whom he addressed by the homely name which Mary had taught him to use in the Nazareth home to Joseph: *Abba*. For Jesus, the thought of God in all his power and glory was softened and blended in the thought of the divine Fatherhood. 'If you then, being evil', he said to his disciples, 'know how to give good gifts to your children, how much more will your heavenly Father give good things to those who ask him' (Matt. 7.11).

Not that Jesus was blind to the terrible in nature. He saw the wolves that devour the flock, the vultures ever ready to swoop down on the carcase. He knew the earthquake and the flood that could sweep away a sand-built house like a cockle shell. Yet these things did not shadow his trust in the goodness of the great Father above. Everywhere in vivid, intense intimacy was the faith that this world, for all its evil and sin, was a room in his Father's house, and with it the kindliness of home.

Now consider the second book in which Jesus read deeply, as St John declares: '[Jesus] knew men so well, all of them, that he needed no evidence from others about a man, for he himself could tell what was in a man' (John 2.25, NEB).

It has often been said that he was the great believer in men. Under no illusions about the evil in our human nature, he yet knew what by God's grace men might become. He who said that men were of 'more value than many sparrows' and that there was joy in heaven when a sinner repented, has rightly been credited with teaching the infinite value of the human soul in God's sight. Jesus had great faith in man – as witness his calling of twelve men, each, it has been said, capable of breaking his heart. He had, moreover, the faculty of discovering interest and worth in unlikely and unlovely people like the woman who was a sinner or the disreputable little inspector of taxes in Jericho. He was never interested in what class people belonged to but in who they were. He was concerned with them as real persons precious to God, potential members of his big family, and therefore to be pitied, and helped, and saved.

Yet, by the same token, he could see into that part of us which makes us right or wrong – the heart (Mark 7.21ff.; Matt. 12.34). Recall how he read the mind and motives of the rich young man or the woman of Samaria and diagnosed their spiritual need; or, again, saw clearly through King Herod's declared interest in himself: 'Go, and tell *that fox*' (Luke 13.32). Jesus cherished no false notions of man's natural goodness. 'If you then, *being evil*', he began his parable of the Asking Son, quietly assuming that ugly twist in our human make-up we call 'sin'.

It is his parables of course which best show with what shrewd discerning eyes Jesus walked amid the human scene. The men and women in them are not puppets but real people, acting in character. Here, for instance, is a wealthy farmer, building still greater barns to house increasing crops, and dreaming of a care-free old age when, suddenly, he drops down dead; and here, at the other end of the scale, is a farm servant who, having done a hard day's work, must fall to and prepare his master's supper before he himself can 'get a bite'. Here, again, is a Sadducee, clad in purple and fine linen and 'faring sumptuously every day'; and there, at his gate, lies poor Lazarus, his body festering with ulcers which the roaming street dogs rasp with their tongues.

Nor does this exhaust the list of real people in the parables. Think of the poor widow whose enemy has refused to settle a lawful debt and who keeps coming daily to the judge 'who feared neither God nor man', demanding justice, until that 'hard' man relents and rewards her importunity. More familiar perhaps are the two men at their prayers in the temple: one thanking God that he is 'not like other men' and pouring the tale of his own righteousness into the ear of omniscience, while the other man, a despised tax-collector, cowers 'afar off', aware that he is a 'rotter' and able only to blurt out, 'God be merciful to me a sinner!' Or recall that resourceful rogue, traditionally named 'the Unjust Steward', who, in a personal crisis, cooked his master's books with his creditors' connivance, and so secured his own future after the dismissal which he foresaw. Above all, think of that story of the Father and his two so very different sons, at once so true to life and yet, in the picture of the gracious Father, how much larger than life!

How unerringly too Jesus reads the characters of those people he encounters during his ministry! Jesus, says T. W. Manson, was never put off by pious humbugs but always brought them back to reality by the shortest possible route. Think of that first-century 'Holy Willie' called Simon (in Luke 7), type of all those 'good' people who (in Reinhold Niebuhr's phrase) 'do not know that they are not "good"'. Or that contentious 'lawyer' (in Luke 10), spoiling for a debate with Jesus about the law, when he asked, 'How can I love my neighbour when I don't know who he really is?', only to be answered, in a story about a hated Samaritan, 'Real love never asks questions like this. All it asks for is opportunities of going into action.' Or consider, finally, that 'theological inquisitive' (the breed is not yet extinct today) who asked Jesus if only a 'few' were going to be 'saved', only to be told in effect, 'It is a case of struggling, not of strolling into God's kingdom. Few enough, my friend, to make you afraid you may not be there. See to your entry!'

All these people in the parables – and how many more – are testimonies to Jesus' knowledge of man in his nobility and his nastiness, and demonstrate how deeply he had read the chequered Book of Human Nature.

We come, last, to the Book of the People of God – the Old Testament.

The gospels reveal Christ's profound knowledge of his people's scripture. He does not handle it like their professional theologians, the Scribes. Indeed, he accuses them of 'neglecting the commandment of God' in favour of 'the tradition of men' (Mark 7.8). He even criticizes Moses' permission of divorce, calling it a concession to human hard-heartedness and pointing men back to God's primal intention in instituting marriage (Mark 10.2-9). Ever he has a way of penetrating to the essential meaning of scripture, as in the Sermon on the Mount (Matt. 5.21-48) he exposes the deepest implications of God's ancient directives to his people.

Moreover, his thought naturally and instinctively clothes itself in scriptural phrase. His chosen name for himself – the Son of man – he probably took from Dan. 7. It is in words from the Psalter and Isaiah that God speaks to him at his baptism. The story of his temptation he phrases – very significantly – in words describing old Israel's 'testing' in the wilderness. In the synagogue at Nazareth, after reading out Isaiah's prediction of the coming time of God's favour (Isa. 61), he declares it to be fulfilled in his ministry. To John the Baptist's question from prison, 'Art thou he that cometh?' he replies in words recalling the promises in Isaiah of God's future day of salvation. From 'the book of Moses' he confutes the Sadducees' disbelief in an afterlife (Mark 12.18-27). By his entry into Jerusalem, his cleansing of the temple and his words to his disciples at the Last Supper he makes explicit the fulfilment of the prophets' (Zechariah and Jeremiah) anticipation in his own person. As in language recalling Hos. 6.2 he predicts his triumph over death (Mark 8.31), so he commits his spirit to God (Luke 23.46) with Ps. 31.5 upon his lips. Above all, in the prophecies of him whom we call 'Second Isaiah' he saw, as in a mirror, his own face and destiny, as the Suffering Servant of the Lord.

One feature in Christ's attitude to his people's scriptures used to trouble earnest believers. He evidently accepted without question the Davidic authorship of the Psalms, ascribed the Pentateuch to Moses, and had no guess that Isa. 40-55 was not the work of Isaiah of Jerusalem. Did it not derogate from his divinity if they had to allow that on such issues Jesus shared the limited knowledge of his contemporaries? Ought he not to have known what, thanks to the 'higher critics', we now know about these matters? So, becoming entangled in Christ's relation to the Old Testament as literature, they missed his relation to it as revelation, and put him at the mercy of critical considerations.

This controversy is now over. Even conservative scholars now freely admit that in this sphere Jesus shared the views of his time, and that, had it been otherwise, there could hardly have been a true incarnation. In literary questions of this sort Jesus never claimed omniscience or infallibility. His knowledge in this field (as on that of the day of the parousia, see Mark 13.32) was in fact limited. What was infallible in Jesus was not the literary views he inherited but his grasp of his heavenly Father and that Father's saving purpose, embodied in himself, for the world. No contemporary ignorance of Christ's about the authorship of the Psalms or the composition of the Pentateuch affects the truth of his witness to God and his gracious designs for sinful men.

We come then to the crucial question: How should we who are Christians read the Old Testament today? The first thing to be said in reply is that today we cannot turn the clock back and seek to read it quite *uncritically*. Historical criticism is here to stay. In the hands of its radical exponents it has doubtless often shaken the faith of simple believers brought up on the doctrine of the Bible as 'the Word incartulate'.

Yet 'criticism', i.e. the scientific study of the Bible, when sanely and constructively employed, is an ally and not an enemy of true Christian faith. It has a necessary and valuable function to perform, even if its place is ancillary –

the handmaid of the gospel, downstairs, not upstairs! For many of us who, in a scientific age, could find no peace of mind in the old theory of the Bible's inspiration, 'higher criticism' has re-discovered the Bible and made of it a new book. (Consider, for example, how Old Testament critics like George Adam Smith have restored the prophets to the church or New Testament critics like C. H. Dodd have illuminated our understanding of the kingdom of God and the parables of Jesus.)

A wise criticism can in fact do two things for us, each of great value. First, by helping us to disengage the kernel from the husk, and discard obsolete weapons and super-fluous baggage, it can clear the way for a house of doctrine in which the component materials can be chosen according to their real strength, and thus enable us to build our Christian *credo* on firm foundations. Second, when such higher criticism is not merely analytic and negative (as earlier it tended to be) but positive and synthetic, it enables us to perceive the fundamental unity of the Bible – to find in the story it tells not a bare chronicle or set of annals but *history with a drift* – the drift of God's ongoing purpose, prefigured in the Old Testament and fulfilled in the New.

We ought then, in our study of the Bible, to avail ourselves of all the help biblical science can give us. But to our study we should bring not only science but 'eyes of faith'. This is only another way of saying that we should approach it as Christ himself did. For him, his Bible – the Old Testament – was a *sacramental* book because it mediated the grace of God in history and pointed forward to that supreme crisis in human affairs in which he knew himself called to play the central and decisive part.

'Christ', says P. T. Forsyth in a fine passage,[3] 'used the Bible as a means of grace, not as a manual of Hebrew or other history ... He found in it the long purpose and deep scope of God's salvation ... He cared little for what our scholars expound – the religion of Israel ... What he found (in the Old Testament) was not the prophets' thoughts of

God but God's invasion of them and their race by words and deeds of gracious power ... *The torch he carried through the Old Testament was the Gospel of grace ...* He read it with the eyes of faith ... and he read it as a whole.'

Is it not our Christian privilege still, while availing ourselves of all the new light provided by the scholars, so to read the Bible? To the study of 'the lively oracles of God' we should bring not only the illumination of modern knowledge but 'eyes of faith'.

NOTES

1. T. T. Lynch.
2. Sir Edwin Arnold.
3. I have abridged the passage. For a full text see M. W. Anderson (ed.), *The Gospel and Authority, a P. T. Forsyth Reader*, Augsburg 1971, pp. 34f.

11

The Meaning of the Cross

The cross, which ended his earthly life, rather than the cradle where it began, holds the secret of our Lord. The cross it was which crowned his mission to men, and of which he cried in triumph before he died, 'It is finished!' (John 19.30), or, as the Greek might equally well be translated, 'the work is done!' Theologians therefore commonly refer to it as 'the work of Christ'.

How did Jesus conceive his work? Before we answer, we must discuss three titles which hold the key to what Jesus was and did: the Son of God, the Son of man, and the Servant of the Lord.

In Jesus' life the supreme reality was his unique relationship to God as Son. Going back, as St Luke tells us (Luke 2.49), to his boyhood this sense of Sonship comes to climactic expression later in his 'Great Thanksgiving' (Matt. 11.27f., Q):

> All things have been delivered to me by my father; and no one knows the Son except the Father, and no one knows the Father except the Son, and anyone to whom the Son chooses to reveal him.

Only to his disciples, however, did Jesus disclose this secret. In public, avoiding the title 'Messiah' because it was fatally loaded with political associations, he chose to be known as 'the Son of man'. Derived from Dan. 7.13ff., it was an enigmatic title, well calculated to conceal, and yet at the same time to reveal to those with ears to hear, his true identity. For, in Aramaic, 'the Son of man' could mean simply 'man' (with a small 'm') or it could mean *the* Man, a messianic figure. On Jesus' lips not only did it contain a veiled claim to be head of the new people of God, but it served to express his kinship with suffering humanity, and it carried also the promise of future triumph for himself and the kingdom which he embodied (cf. Dan. 7.13f. with Mark 14.62).

It was another Old Testament figure – Isaiah's Servant of the Lord – and especially Isa. 53 – which showed Jesus the way, appointed by his Father, which he must travel, if his 'work' were to be done.

So to the story of Jesus' ministry among men which is, at the same time, the tale of a traffic between two worlds, the unseen and the seen. It begins at Jordan when, identifying himself with sinners, Jesus submits to John's baptism. Note, in Mark's account of it (Mark 1.9-13), how Jewish images are used to express heavenly realities which, though imperceptible to outward eye and ear, are utterly real.

As Jesus rose from the waters, he saw the heavens opened and the Spirit, like a dove, descending on him. Came a voice from heaven, 'Thou art my beloved (or only) Son; with thee I am well pleased.'

The Spirit's descent means that Jesus knows himself to be equipped with God's power for his work (cf. Isa. 42.1, 'I have put my Spirit upon him'). The heavenly voice echoes the coronation formula of the messianic king of Israel (Ps. 2.7; cf. Gen. 22.2), as the phrase 'with thee I am well pleased' echoes the ordination formula of the Servant of the Lord ('my chosen, in whom I delight').

The dominant motifs here are sonship and service. What Jesus received in this momentous experience was an inner authentication of his divine sonship, and his Father's call to be a Messiah patterned on Isaiah's Servant of the Lord, who was to be 'a light to all peoples, a beacon for the nations' (Isa. 42.6, NEB).

The news that Herod had imprisoned his great fore-runner was for Jesus the signal to begin his appointed work.

Into Galilee he came, announcing to his countrymen that God's reign, for whose coming they had long prayed, was now 'upon them' and men must turn back to God and believe the good news. With authority he taught in the synagogues; in the towns he wrought miracles of healing. His fame rang through all Galilee. But his consorting with sinners, his claim to forgive sins, and his 'cavalier' attitude to the sabbath so shocked the Jewish churchman that, to continue his work, he had to leave the synagogues for the lakeside. Thus Jesus spear-headed his great campaign, the kingdom of God against the powers of evil, as by parable he challenged men with the kingdom's claims and by miracles of mercy he manifested its presence.

Twelve men whom he had chosen and trained to be the nucleus of the new Israel, he now sent forth to proclaim God's inbreaking kingdom by word and by deed. Such was the excitement following his missionaries' return that thousands flocked after Jesus to the north end of the lake, and there in a desert spot he fed them – fed them with the bread of the kingdom. It was the Galilean Lord's Supper. He had come, as he said, to invite not the righteous but sinners to the banquet of God's kingdom (Mark 2.17); and there he was now doing it – acting out his own parable of the Great Supper (Luke 14), hoping greatly that, by their response, the Galileans would align themselves with God's high purpose for Israel embodied in himself.

Alas, by their reaction, the five thousand men (*andres*) showed how earthbound were their ideas of God's kingdom. As John 6.15 shows, what they were dreaming of was a 'revolt in the desert'[1] against hated Rome, with Jesus as their leader.

Long before Jesus had rejected this kind of Messiahship as a very temptation of the devil (Matt. 4.8-10, Q). So now, briefly, he escaped from the dangerous enthusiasm of his followers, outside of Galilee, that in quiet communion with his Father he might learn the divine will for himself. By the time he and the twelve had reached Caesarea Philippi, he knew. Messiah he was, as Peter now confessed him to be, but a Messiah who must (*dei*) as the Lord's Servant go to his throne by way of a gibbet (Mark 8.31). 'Your Messiah', he told the protesting Peter, 'is a conqueror. God's Messiah is a servant.' If God's kingdom were to 'come with power' (Mark 9.1), a *via dolorosa* stretched out before him and his men.

The time had come when he must carry the challenge and crisis of God's kingdom into the very home and heart of Jewry. So the march southwards on Jerusalem began....

Followed a ministry of some three months in Jerusalem in which Jesus challenged Sadducees and Pharisees alike with the divine crisis now overhanging Israel, and in parables summoned the people to repent before it was too late. As the high-priest Caiaphas told his colleagues (John 11.47-53), it had now become a choice between the death of this troubler in Israel and the ruin of their nation. This crisis Jesus met, as he had met the earlier one in Galilee, by withdrawing – this time from Jerusalem across the Jordan. There, in the peace of Perea, his purpose crystallized in the decision to go back to Jerusalem at Passover time and finish the work God had given him to do.[2]

Now ensued all the events we associate with Holy Week: the entry in lowly pomp into the Holy City, the cleansing of the temple, the priests' plot and the betrayal, the arrest and the trial, the crucifixion and the burial.... For a moment in Gethsemane he seemed to hesitate, and there was an hour of agony. But on he went, past all our power to follow him, even in thought, on to the end of the road marked out for the Servant Messiah, and, by and by, on an April Sunday morning (7 April, AD 30?) came back in glory with blessing on his lips and on his face unshadowed peace.

*   *   *

Concerning Jesus' passion it has been rightly said that he was a traveller by faith (*viator*) rather than one who clearly sees the end from the beginning (*comprehensor*).

Nonetheless, on the way which took Jesus and his disciples from Galilee to Golgotha, he gave them hint after pregnant hint of the purpose of his mission and the blessings it would bring.

'I have a baptism to undergo', he said (Luke 12.50; Mark 10.38). His passion was a 'baptism' *in blood* which would cleanse men from their sin. Again, it was a 'cup' of suffering which his Father had given him to drink, so that there might be set up a 'new covenant' between God and men (Mark 10.38; 14.23f.; I Cor. 11.25). Once, Jesus compared his passion to a road to be travelled: 'the Son of Man', he said, 'is going the way appointed for him in the scriptures' (Mark 14.21, NEB). Not far from journey's end he told his disciples, 'The Son of man came not to be served but to serve and to give his life as a ransom for many' (Mark 10.45, where 'many' is Hebrew for 'all', i.e. for the common salvation). His death was the price that must be paid if they were to be delivered from the doom which overhung them.

A baptism to be undergone, a cup to be drunk, a road to be travelled, a price to be paid – so, by one vivid metaphor after another, did Jesus signal at the meaning of his work before he finished it on the cross.

Here it is worth stopping to reflect that, if the disciples' last glimpse had been of their Master on his cross, these passion sayings of his we have been quoting would never have been remembered, nor indeed would he himself. With the death of Jesus there died also his disciples' faith in him. It was the resurrection which changed everything – taught them to see the cross not as stark tragedy brought about by men who knew not what they did, but as God's way of rescuing men from their sins. What the first Easter Day (and those that followed) showed the disciples was that God no less than man was at work in the apparent *débâcle* of the cross. The resurrection was God's guarantee of the redemption won upon the cross.

Followed, fifty days later, Pentecost; and the disciples, their minds now illumined by the promised Holy Spirit, began to think out the meaning of the cross. Half a dozen years later (as Paul tells us in I Cor. 15.3) they had set down their finding: 'Christ died for our sins according to the scriptures'. Chief among these 'scriptures' must have been the chapter which tells of God's Servant who 'bore the sin of many' (Isa. 53.12).

'Christ in his apostles interpreted his finished work as truly as in his life-time he interpreted his unfinished work.'[3] How did they begin? The cross, they said, was no tragic accident. It had happened 'by the deliberate will and plan of God' (Acts 2.23, NEB). When we find Peter, the leader in the infant church, calling Christ 'God's Servant' (Acts 3.13, 26; 4.27, 30), we perceive he has now grasped the truth from which, at Caesarea Philippi (Mark 8.32), he had recoiled in horror: then, for him, a suffering Messiah had been a thing unthinkable.[4]

Yet among the apostles it was not Peter the rough fisherman but Paul the trained thinker who penetrated most deeply into the meaning of the cross. Once (Rom. 3.25), he says that Christ crucified has become for all men what the 'mercy seat' (*hilasterion*) symbolized for old Israel (Ex. 25.17f.). What was once figured forth on the Day of Atonement (Lev. 16) has been fulfilled in Christ. The cross is the place where God shows his mercy to all mankind. Yet perhaps Paul's profoundest word on it comes in II Cor. 5.21: 'Christ was innocent of sin, and yet for our sake God made him one with the sinfulness of men, so that in him we might be made one with the goodness of God himself' (NEB). What can this mean but that the cross was a deed wherein, by God's appointing, our condemnation came upon the sinless Christ that there might for us be condemnation no more (Rom. 8.1)? In being 'made sin' Christ took sin in its whole reality upon himself, as once, for old Israel, the hapless scapegoat was thought to do.

Now turn to St John. For him, the cross is the supreme proof of God's love (John 3.16), as it means the defeat of the powers of evil (John 12.31). Christ's death is necessary if men are to win the 'eternal life' which he comes to bring (John 3.16; 10.10; 12.24). For the Son of God appears in order to destroy the works of the devil (I John 3.8); he 'dies to make men holy' (John 17.19); and, by cleansing them from sin's defilement, makes possible their forgiveness (I John 2.2; 4.10).

Likewise, for the writer to the Hebrews, sin creates the barrier between men and holy God. Its remover is Jesus, our great and merciful High Priest (4.14-5.10). This he does, once for all, by the sacrifice of his own sinless life in obedience to God's will, thereby opening up for us 'a new and living way' into the Holy of Holies, which is heaven (Heb. 7-10).

Finally, at the New Testament's end, John the Seer of Patmos speaks for all early Christians in his doxology to the crucified and living Christ: 'Now to him who loves us and has loosed us from our sins by his own blood' (Rev. 1.5).

So, through the apostolic writings runs one mighty thought: Christ died for our sins, bore what we should have borne, did for God what was God's good pleasure, did for us what we could never have done for ourselves.

Theology is simply faith thinking – faith giving a reasoned account of itself. From post-apostolic days to our own the best minds of the church have wrestled with the meaning of the cross. To what conclusions have they come?

All have agreed that *the cross reveals the love of God.* Yet, if we take this to be the whole truth, we fall short of the mind of Christ who knew himself called not simply to reveal God's love but, as God's 'apostle', to *do* for men something they could never do for themselves.

So, second, our theologians have agreed with the apostles that *Christ bore our sins*. But how? By so identifying himself with our race that he entered with us and for us into the divine judgment which must ever rest on human sin. The cup which Jesus had to drink was 'the cup our sins had mingled'. This too was what underlay his agony in Gethsemane and that cry of dereliction (Mark 15.34) when, as the burden of the world's sin which he was carrying, seemed, for the time of his passion, to wall him off from his Father.

Some have said that in all this God was 'punishing' Jesus for our sakes and in our stead. Were a human judge so to allow an innocent man to be punished for another's crime, we should not hesitate to call him 'unjust'. No more then should we so describe God's treatment of a Son who was ever well-pleasing to him.

'Penal' Christ's sufferings were, but only in the sense that in his passion he had to endure on men's behalf the divine reaction against the sin of the human race to whom, as the Son of man, he had betrothed himself, for better, for worse. Let us think of the suffering which good men often endure when they deeply love wrong-doers, and we may surmise how Jesus felt as he went to the cross. We may also perceive that, in so identifying himself with sinners, he was honouring the holiness of God who, just because of his love for them, cannot palter with sin but must deal with it decisively, if men are to be forgiven.

Even so, we have not yet said what is perhaps the highest thing ever said about the cross. Since, in the Christian view, 'the Judge of all the earth' is revealed as a holy heavenly Father who wills that his wayward children should return to their Father's house, no law-court language can adequately set forth the full meaning of the cross. Legal categories must give way to personal ones.

If we adopt them, we may see Christ in his work as *the great confessor of our sins before his Father*. So, in his *Nature of the Atonement* (1856), John McLeod Campbell read the riddle of the cross. Christ, he said, as our representative, offered on the cross a perfect confession of our sins, a confession which could be described as 'a perfect Amen in humanity to the judgment of God on the sin of man'. To the divine wrath against it, he responded, on man's behalf, 'Righteous art Thou, O Lord, who judgest so'. And by that perfect response he absorbed it, so making possible our forgiveness by holy God.[5]

If someone objects, 'Nobody can confess sin but the sinner. How then could the sinless Christ confess our sins?' we may reply, 'A human mother can make her own the sin of her child, and could not Christ have done this for the race he came to save?' If the sin of other people can be so felt, it can also be confessed, not indeed as our own, but as that of those whom we love.

But we may go even further. People are not separate entities like pebbles on a beach. We are all bound up together in the bundle of life. Nowadays we are realizing afresh something which was patent to Paul long ago, namely, the truly *corporate* nature of sin. Willy nilly, we are all caught up in the mesh of the world's wickedness. Moral man, as Reinhold Niebuhr said, finds himself entangled in an immoral society.

Thus we may understand how Christ, though himself sinless, had, in becoming man, so deeply involved himself in our sin as well as in our human situation, that from the inside (as it were) he could perfectly confess men's sins to his Father.

We do well then to see in the cross the revelation of God's love for sinners. We do better to think of the atonement as an act in which Christ entered with us and for us into God's judgment on sin, so removing the barrier which separated us from him. We do best of all, with McLeod Campbell, to think of Christ as representing us before his Father and making, as only he could make, the perfect confession of our sins, thus enabling us, in Paul's phrase, to be 'accepted in the beloved' (Eph. 1.6).

You and I (to use a homely parable) are like the boy who has misbehaved and been sent to his room in disgrace. There he sits, sullen and resentful. Suddenly he becomes aware of his elder brother in the room, sharing his disgrace. 'Surely *he* hasn't done wrong?' he muses. Then on his elder brother's face he sees a look which he cannot quite fathom. It almost looks as if his elder brother were really glad to be there. Then the elder brother invites him to go back to their father. The boy refuses. Thereupon the elder brother says: 'All is forgiven. Father will take you back, for my sake.' So, shamefacedly, the boy goes. But, when he enters his father's presence, he catches the same look on the father's face which he had seen on his brother's. And the father takes the boy in his arms and forgives him.

Such is Christ's work *for* us. Yet, to be effective, it must also become Christ's work *in* us. And this it becomes when we respond to it in humble faith, when round the sacramental table we partake of 'Christ's love-tokens to his body, the church', and when in our day-by-day living we seek to serve our fellow-men in love, for his dear sake.

Our forefathers spoke much of 'the finished work of Christ', and rightly. In principle, the world has been redeemed: the thing is done, it is not to do. In a true sense, the cross was the last judgment: 'Now is the judgment of this world, now shall the ruler of this world be cast out' (John 12.31). Yet no doctrine of the atonement is complete which has not a 'forward-look'. The redemption once wrought on the cross remains to be worked out until it covers all humanity and, as the early Christians sang, 'at the name of Jesus every knee shall bow' (Phil. 2.10).

We have been trying to summarize Christian thought about Christ's work. No doctrine of atonement may claim to express the whole truth of that act whereby God in Christ took the responsibility of evil upon himself and somehow subsumed it under good. Wisely therefore the church universal has never required subscription to any one doctrine of the atonement as necessary for saving faith.

The Meaning of the Cross

In its prayers and praises down the centuries it has continued to affirm the fact:

O Saviour of the world, who by thy Cross and precious blood hast redeemed us.

Yet this does not mean that Christians have considered the death of Christ to be a fact shrouded in impenetrable mystery. On the contrary, like the apostles, they have discovered profound meaning in the cross; and it was given to an Irish woman, Cecil Frances Alexander, in a hymn she wrote for children, to express better than many a learned tome, the purpose, the necessity and the challenge of that sacrifice which has in principle redeemed our prodigal human race:

He died that we might be forgiven,
    He died to make us good,
That we might go at last to heaven,
    Saved by his precious blood.

There was no other good enough
    To pay the price of sin,
He only could unlock the gate
    Of heaven and let us in.

O dearly, dearly has he loved,
    And we must love him too,
And trust in his redeeming blood,
    And try his works to do.

NOTES

1. Such a 'revolt in the Judean desert' did in fact occur about a hundred years later under a Messianic pretender calling himself Bar Cochba ('Son of a Star'). Rome ruthlessly suppressed it.

2. On the historicity of the Jerusalem ministry and the withdrawal across Jordan, see my *Works and Words of Jesus*, revised edition, SCM Press 1973, pp. 132-38.

3. P. T. Forsyth, *The Person and Place of Jesus Christ*, Independent Press 1948, p. 60.

4. Cf. I Peter 2.21-25 where the crucified Christ is set forth as the Suffering Servant of the Lord (Isa. 53).

5. Of McLeod Campbell's book James Denney said: 'He walks in light all the time.' *The Christian Doctrine of Reconciliation*, 1917, p. 120.

12

The Resurrection

'The only God the New Testament knows anything about,'
William Manson of Edinburgh used to say, 'is the God of
the resurrection.' The resurrection of Christ is in fact the
diamond pivot on which the whole truth of Christianity
turns. If the disciples' fellowship with their Master ended
on the cross, the gospel is a nonsense and our faith an
empty husk. If the resurrection is true, if by raising Christ
from the dead God set his seal upon the Son of man's
sacrifice, why then, as Browning says,

> ... But Easter-Day breaks! But
> Christ rises! Mercy every way
> Is infinite, – and who can say?[1]

the divine love which took Christ to the cross (Rom. 5.8)
is shown to be not only merciful but mighty, and we can
make our own Paul's great conviction that neither death
nor life nor anything else in all creation can separate us
from God's love in Christ (Rom. 8.31-39).

Let us study the resurrection first as fact, then as experience, and finally as hope.

First, as *historical fact*.
Here let us frankly acknowledge the great service historical
criticism can render us. For it can help us to separate kernel
from husk and (changing the metaphor) save time so often
lost in the defence of outposts. In the case of the resurrection
this means that criticism enables us to sift out the strongest
historical evidence for this unique event, and thus clears
the way for building Christian belief in the risen Christ
on the firmest possible foundations. We shall therefore

concentrate on what, by the judgment of the experts, are the two oldest and best pieces of evidence at our disposal, namely, eight verses from our earliest New Testament writer, St Paul, and eight verses from the earliest gospel, Mark.

The New Testament, observe, contains two distinct strands of evidence for the resurrection. We have (*a*) testimony to various appearances of the risen Lord to his disciples, and (*b*) testimony to the fact that on the first Easter Day three women found his rock-tomb empty. The earliest account of the appearances is, as we propose to show, that contained in I Cor. 15.3-8. The earliest account of the finding of the empty tomb is that in Mark 16.1-8. Let us study them in turn.

(1) I Cor. 15.3-8.

> First and foremost, I handed on to you the facts which had been imparted to me: that Christ died for our sins in accordance with the scriptures; that he was buried; that he was raised to life on the third day, according to the scriptures; and that he appeared to Cephas, and afterwards to the Twelve. Then he appeared to over five hundred of our brothers at once, most of whom are still alive, though some have died. Then he appeared to James, and afterwards to all the apostles.
>
> In the end he appeared even to me (NEB).

Most of this passage represents pre-Pauline Christian 'tradition', that is, something which Paul himself 'received' from his Christian predecessors. Its style strongly suggests a very early Christian summary of 'things most surely believed' and that, as Paul says (I Cor. 15.11) by all the apostles. Six appearances of Christ are listed: three to individuals, three to groups of people. The appearance to more than five hundred 'brothers' cannot be equated, as some have suggested, with the multitude on the Day of Pentecost (Acts 2), since no appearance of the risen Christ is there recorded. 'Most of whom are still alive, though some have died' is Paul's added comment. Among 'all the apostles', a different group from the twelve, we should probably include men like Barnabas, Andronicus and

Junias (Rom. 16.7). 'In the end he appeared even to me'
refers of course to the Damascus road experience.

Where and when did Paul get this 'tradition'? Either
in Damascus after his conversion (generally dated AD 33);
or during his first visit to Jerusalem after his conversion
(see Gal. 1.18f.) i.e. in AD 35 or 36. For two reasons the
latter is likelier: (*a*) The text contains numerous
'Semitisms' – Jewish idioms glimmering through the Greek
and pointing to Jerusalem as place of origin.[2] (*b*) The two
apostles named by Paul in I Cor. 15.3ff., namely, Peter
and James the Lord's brother, are precisely the two whom
Paul says he met on his historic visit to the mother church.

Here then is traditional testimony to the fact of the
resurrection taking us back to within half a dozen years of
the crucifixion, and it has rightly been called 'the oldest
document of the Christian church which we possess.'[3]
Moreover, it is 'tradition' whose *truth was open to testing*.
When Paul wrote, Peter and James were still living and
most of the 'five hundred brethren' yet survived and could
be questioned. The passage therefore preserves uniquely
early and verifiable testimony. It meets every reasonable
demand of historical reliability. Doubt this 'tradition' and
you might as well doubt everything else in the New
Testament.

(2) Alongside this tradition we have to set the separate
testimony to the empty tomb, found in its earliest form
in Mark 16.1-8.

Scholars now agree that the passion was the first part of
the story of Jesus to be put down in connected form –
probably years before AD 50, to judge from the 'traditional'
account of the Lord's Supper (I Cor. 11.23ff.) which is
set in the context of 'the night of his arrest'. Mark 16.1-8
rests back therefore on just such an account of how Jesus
met his death, as its climax and conclusion was the story
of the discovery of the empty tomb.[4]

Various features argue the historical reliability of Mark

16.1-8. In its favour is the sheer starkness of the preceding account of how Jesus died in utter loneliness. Next, if it had not in fact been true, no Jew would have made three women, and not disciples, the first recipients of the news that the grave was empty: women's witness was not highly regarded.[5] Verse 3 ('They were wondering among themselves who would roll away the stone') suggests their vividly remembered anxiety. The statement in verse 6 that they fled from the gaping tomb in 'numinous terror' was surely never fabricated. In fact, save for the mention of 'the young man' at the tomb (commonly supposed to be an angel, though thought by some to be Mark) the narrative is singularly free of fantastic features. What it does suggest is the awefulness and mystery of the sight that met the women's gaze. 'If we test what is here capable of being tested,' says the German historian von Campenhausen,[6] 'we cannot shake Mark's story of the empty tomb.'

The earliest forms of these two strands of tradition therefore inspire great confidence. The other important point to seize is that they *originated independently*.[7] The story of the empty tomb in Mark 16 does not record an appearance of the risen Lord, and concerns not disciples but women. On the other hand, the record of Christ's appearances in I Cor. 15 had originally no connexion with the locality of the grave. Granted to disciples, the appearances were in the nature of calls to apostolic mission. Thus our two independent strands of historical evidence complement and confirm each other, and show that our belief in the resurrection is rooted not in fantasy but in historic fact.

This evidence however does not stand alone. There are three corroborative witnesses to its truth.

First, the existence of the Christian church. Had the crucifixion ended the disciples' fellowship with Jesus, it is hard to see how the church could ever have come into existence, and harder still to explain how it has lasted nearly two thousand years.

Second, the existence of the New Testament. Who would have troubled to write these twenty-seven books if Jesus had ended his career on the cross? Every written record about him was made by men who believed in a risen Lord.

Third, the existence of the Lord's day. No Christian Jew would have changed the sacred day from sabbath (Saturday) to 'the first day of the week' (Acts 20.7; I Cor. 16.2; Rev. 1.10) except for the reason that on this day Jesus was known to have conquered death. Every Lord's day is a weekly witness to the reality of the resurrection.

We have now to consider the earliest evidence for the *nature* of the resurrection.

I Cor. 15 shows us what Paul believed. He declares that a change from a 'natural' to a 'spiritual' (or 'heavenly') body is the appointed destiny of the Christian believer, and since he calls Christ 'the first-fruits of those who have fallen asleep', he plainly believed the same wonderful change to have come over Christ's body: his 'lowly' body had become 'the body of glory' (Phil. 3.21).

Now since in I Cor. 15.1-8 Paul ranks his sight of the risen Lord with that of Peter and the others, we are entitled to infer that they held the same view. For them, Jesus was already in heaven, and from there in his glorified body he had manifested himself to them.

It is but another way of making the same point to say that for the earliest Christians the resurrection and the ascension were not two events but one. Only in Acts 1 do we have scriptural warrant for the church's scheme of forty days (a traditional number) between resurrection and ascension. In the pre-Pauline hymn of Phil. 2.6-11 'highly exalted' signifies resurrection plus ascension, and nowhere in his letters does Paul refer to the ascension as a separate event.

To be sure, in some of the gospel stories about the risen Christ he is said to have taken food and drink. These statements were surely meant to defend the disciples against the charge that they had seen a ghost. Yet even in stories which contain such corporeal details, Jesus appears as *already exalted*, as one who can come through closed doors, and appear and disappear.

From the earliest evidence we therefore conclude that Christ left the grave 'incorruptibly', his earthly body having been transmuted into a 'heavenly' one.

What, finally, did the fact of the resurrection mean for the first Christians? On the day of Pentecost, Peter said: 'Let all Israel accept as certain that God made this Jesus, whom you crucified, both Lord and Messiah' (Acts 2.36). The resurrection meant divine vindication for their Master. It was God's 'Yes' to his 'finished work' (John 19.30). More, as Paul saw and said, it was proof that divine love was on the throne of the universe (cf. Rom. 5.11 with 8.31-39).

Yet this is only half the truth. For pious Jews in the first century AD, 'the resurrection of the dead' signified the great hope of the end-time when God would wind up the scroll of history and there would come the Last Judgment. But if Jesus had been raised from the dead, then in one man – the Son of man and the cause he embodied – that end had been marvellously anticipated. The first Christians felt themselves to be living in a new age, as that one vacant tomb in the wide graveyard of the world was the 'first instalment' (*arrabōn*) of God's great future for his people.

Note. It has been made a count against the truth of the resurrection that those to whom Christ appeared were believers, not neutral witnesses. Believers they were not. So far from being buoyed up in faith, they were sunk in despair and received the first tidings of it as 'idle tales' (Luke 24.11). The truth is that those to whom Christ appeared became *believers*. In their encounters with the risen Lord they were confronted, overwhelmed and claimed by Christ.

The fact of the resurrection does not however stand alone. We have to reckon with the *experience* – men's experience, down nineteen centuries, of the living Christ.

If, as we have seen, the risen Christ did not return to his former life, he did not forsake his followers. 'No apostle – no New Testament writer – ever *remembered* Christ', said Denney.[8] They had no need to. Through the Holy Spirit – Christ's *alter ego*, sent not so much to supply Christ's absence as to accomplish his presence – he was still with them, as the book of Acts shows. They felt themselves to be sharing in this risen life.

Paul's letters show what is meant. 'All I care for', he wrote to the Philippians, 'is to experience the power of his resurrection' (Phil. 3.10). Since 'you are risen with Christ', he commanded the Colossians, 'seek the things which are above where Christ is, seated at the right hand of God' (Col. 3.1). St John's language may be different; but when he writes about 'eternal life' as a *present* possession – as in John 5.24; 11.25; I John 3.14; 5.12 – it is to the same experience that he refers.

This is what is meant by Christ's resurrection as an experience; nor is it one shared only by the first Christians. From Polycarp of Smyrna to David Livingstone of Blantyre, from the Spanish saint Teresa to the Indian Sadhu Sundar Singh, from Dr Dale of Birmingham to Charles Raven of Cambridge, from Sir Wilfred Grenfell of Labrador to the heroic Dietrich Bonhoeffer of Hitler's Germany – and how many more unknown to fame or the history books! – the testimony has been ever the same: 'Christ is alive! He has had dealings with us, and we with him.' Listen to the poet:[9]

> Shakespeare is dust and will not come
> To question from his Avon tomb,
> And Socrates and Shelley keep
> An Attic and Italian sleep . . .
>
> They see not. But O Christians who
> Throng Holburn and Fifth Avenue,
> May you not meet, in spite of death,
> A traveller from Nazareth?

Nay more, have not most of us known men and women in whom the Spirit of the risen Christ is now manifestly at work? Already they have risen above the darkness of doubt, the tyranny of self and all the pettiness of life, above all fear for the future. By their very lives they make the fact of the resurrection credible today. They know that their redeemer lives and that they are 'risen with him', even in this life.

Finally, the resurrection is a hope – our hope founded on the fact of the living Christ. Because he lives, we too may hope to live also (John 14.19).

None spells out the theology of this hope more fully than St Paul (I Thess. 4; I Cor. 15; II Cor. 5; Rom. 8). We may sum it up in two verses:

> Since we believe that Jesus died and rose again, even so through Jesus, God will bring with him those who have fallen asleep (I Thess. 4.14).
> If the Spirit of him who raised Jesus from the dead dwells in you, he who raised Christ from the dead will give life to your mortal bodies through his Spirit which dwells in you (Rom. 8.11).

Our 'mortal bodies', observe. Not so very long ago the very idea of the resurrection of the *body* was a stumbling-block not only to unbelievers but to Christians who, preferring Plato to Paul, set their hope on the immortality of the *soul*, which, as John Baillie pointed out, is but a philosophical version of the primitive, animistic sense of a shadowy survival of death.[10] Nowadays, with the recovery of a truer biblical view and the abandonment of a rigid antithesis between spirit and matter, the wheel has turned and the once despised phrase, 'I believe in the resurrection of the body' is seen to conserve the very genius of the Christian faith.

Today philosophers, psychologists and doctors alike repudiate the dichotomizing of man into body and soul and regard him as a unity. At the same time, our latest theologians (e.g. Pannenberg) remind us that, though the word 'resurrection' comes from the weird world of Jewish apocalyptic, it is really an everyday metaphor derived from the familiar experience of *awakening* to the life of a new day, and that for the Jews it was a parable of the destiny appointed for God's people at the end-time (Dan. 12.2; Isa. 26.19). Moreover, unlike some of our Christian ancestors who believed in a 'resurrection of relics', we have taken to heart Paul's statement, 'Flesh and blood cannot inherit the kingdom of God' (I Cor. 15.50), and realize that what he teaches is a resurrection not of *matter* but of *form*. (For the apostle, the *sōma*, or 'body' is the principle of individuation or identity which persists through all changes of substance, so that 'the spiritual body' which God will give the faithful when their great 'transformation' comes, will be one in which the fullness of personality is preserved.)

According to the Christian view, then, immortality is the gift of God in Christ. (We have no Christian warrant for the view that man was *created* immortal.) The Christian hope is that those who now are 'in Christ' – grafted by faith into him as the twig is grafted into the living tree – will one day be 'with Christ' in his glory. As on the first Easter Day God raised his Son from the sleep of death and raised him to heaven, so, in his appointed time, he will rouse from sleep those who are Christ's, and they will arise and make their abode with him for ever in his Father's house (John 14.2). Indeed, the Christian's final destiny is nothing less than Christlikeness. We are to be 'shaped to the likeness of his Son' says St Paul (Rom. 8.29, NEB). 'We shall be like him', writes St John, 'for we shall see him as he is' (I John 3.2).

The Christian hope is therefore completely, even dominically, ethical. Diverse have been the pictures painted of the afterlife – some crude, some carnal, some senti-mental. The apostles hold fast what is characteristically Christian. Salvation, full and final, means sharing the likeness of our Lord, the Father's first-born from the dead.

The Resurrection

Let us end with the note on which we began – the importance of the resurrection for Christian faith. A modern German scholar[11] has memorably summed it up:

> It is Easter which shows us that God and his love for his errant creatures are both invincible; for it is at Easter that God, who has no need or conceivable obligation to do any such thing, gives back to men the Christ they had rejected, the Christ who died and is now alive for ever more.

NOTES

1. Robert Browning, 'Easter Day'.
2. J. Jeremias, *The Eucharistic Words of Jesus*, SCM Press 1966, p. 102.
3. E. Meyer, *Ursprung und Anfänge des Christentums*, Berlin 1921, p. 210.
4. U. Wilckens, *Auferstehung*, Stuttgart 1970, pp. 55f.
5. 'Sooner let the words of the law be burnt', said one rabbi, 'than be delivered to women.'
6. H. von Campenhausen, *Tradition and Life in the Church*, Collins 1968, p. 77.
7. Later there was a tendency to draw the two strands closer together – as witness Matt. 28.8ff. where the discovery of the empty tomb is immediately followed by an appearance of the risen Christ.
8. James Denney, *Studies in Theology*, 1894, p. 154.
9. John Drinkwater.
10. John Baillie, *And the Life Everlasting*, 1934, ch. 4.
11. K. H. Rengstorf in his *Die Auferstehung Jesu*, Witten-Ruhr 1960.

13

The Person of Christ

'What think ye of Christ?' An old question but an ever new one. How are we to explain one who dominates the New Testament and has inspired the lives of Christians for nigh two thousand years?

Shall we content ourselves with calling him prophet, hero, or humanity at its highest?

Or, going a step further, shall we call him superman – half god but still a creature?

Or – regarding this as but a half-way house – shall we with the organ voice of Christendom at large, call him not superman but supernal man – the God-man, our man from heaven and now in heaven?

If we are to reach a satisfactory answer, the evidence to be considered is three-fold:

(1) The Jesus of the gospels;
(2) The testimony of the apostles;
(3) The voice of Christian experience.

We start with the gospels. Did Jesus regard himself merely as the herald of God's good news about his kingdom, or did he believe himself to be a part of it?

Last century it was the view of Liberal Protestants generally that the gospel, as proclaimed by Jesus, had to do with the Father, not with himself.[1] He was the great prophet of God's Fatherhood. Through their failure to grasp what the kingdom of God in the gospels really meant, they had failed to perceive that Jesus is quite central to the good news which he preached.

Thanks to our better understanding of eschatology, we now know that the kingdom of God means God in his sovereign grace invading history in the ministry of Jesus, in order to visit and redeem his people. Nor can we study Jesus' teaching about that kingdom, in which the king in the kingdom is a Father, without perceiving that Jesus himself is the living embodiment of the gospel he proclaimed. It is not only that in this or that saying of his he conjoins the kingdom with his own person (e.g. Luke 11.20); it is that the kingdom is promised only to those who follow him. Where Jesus is, the kingdom is. To be discipled to Jesus is to be 'in the kingdom'. Accordingly, a great modern theologian like Barth can join hands, across the centuries, with an ancient heretic like Marcion, in affirming that 'in the gospel the kingdom of God is Christ himself'. Near the end of his life Barth was asked in a television interview, 'Has your conception of Christ's person changed over the years?' 'Yes', he answered, 'at the beginning I thought Jesus was the prophet of the kingdom. Now I know that he *is* the kingdom.'

Consider the parables (which are all, in one way or another, parables of the kingdom) because in no part of the gospel tradition can we be surer we are in direct contact with the mind of the historic Jesus. (And let us bear in mind, when studying them, that Jesus deliberately refused to call himself the Messiah, or Christ, because that title was fatally burdened with misleading political connotations.)

'When a parable speaks about the kingdom of God', says Ernst Fuchs, 'Jesus is hidden behind the kingdom as its secret content.'[2] He means that in the parables, if we have ears to hear, we shall find 'implicit christology' – veiled hints of what he claimed to be. This applies to the parables of the lost in Luke 15, to those of the Apprenticed Son and the True Shepherd in John's gospel (John 5.19f.;

10.1-5), and to the Two Builders, the wicked Tenants and the Last Judgment. It is true also of the parables of crisis which Jesus uttered on his way to Jerusalem where (as C. W. F. Smith has shown) we see Jesus as the central figure and precipitant of the great crisis in his ministry which culminated in the cross, saying things which none short of the Messiah had the right to say and knowing himself to be, under God, the sole bearer of Israel's destiny.[3]

This however is only the beginning of the evidence. The gospels preserve not a few quite incontestably genuine sayings of Jesus which imply that with his coming the reign of God has dawned. Think of his words in the synagogue at Nazareth, 'Today this scripture (Isa. 61) has been fulfilled in your hearing' (Luke 4.16-21); or his reply to the Baptist's question from prison, 'Go and tell John what you have seen and heard' (Luke 7.18-23), or his 'makarism' to the disciples, 'Blessed are the eyes which see what you see! For I tell you that many prophets and kings desired to see what you see and did not see it, and to hear what you hear, and did not hear it' (Luke 10.23f.).

Add to these his many 'Amen I tell you' utterances instinct with an awareness of being the bearer of God's kingdom to men and of speaking 'as his Father had bidden him'; or his use of the sovereign 'I' (*ego*) in the Sermon on the Mount and elsewhere; or those 'I came' sayings pregnant with an extraordinary sense of his divine mission (e.g. Mark 2.17; Matt. 5.17; Luke 12.49). Above all, lay account with his 'Great Thanksgiving' (Matt. 11.25ff.) in which Jesus claims to be the Son of God in a lonely and unshared sense and the sole mediator to men of this knowledge of God.

Yet a study of his words does not disclose to us the total Christ of the gospels. For there came a time in his ministry when words were no longer of any avail, when only a deed could effect what his Father had sent him into the world to do. 'The cross and not the cradle holds the secret of the Lord', and perhaps the most remarkable self-revelation of all Jesus reserved for an upper room on the last night of his earthly life. 'This is my body' is remarkable enough, yet even more so is his word over the cup, whether you accept Paul's version of it, 'This cup is the new covenant in my blood' (I Cor. 11.25) or Mark's, 'This is my blood of the covenant which is poured out for many' (Mark 14.24). Centuries before, at the very nadir of his people's fortunes, Jeremiah had seen their only hope of salvation in God's making with them a 'new covenant' not in stone but in the heart of man: in that day all would know God, he would forgive their sins, and they would be truly his people (Jer. 31.31ff.). Then what manner of man is this who knows that by his death he will inaugurate this new and blessed order of relations between God and men? Only men who dismiss the gospel record as a tissue of fables can avoid the conclusion to which all this evidence points: *Jesus was central to the gospel which he proclaimed.*

Before we turn to the apostles, a word on kingdom, cross and resurrection.

Since the kingdom was initiated in the ministry of Jesus, we may not say that he died to bring in the kingdom. The cross must fall *within* the kingdom, form its burning focus and centre – the climactic deed in the warfare of God against the kingdom of evil. If then the cross is the end which crowns Jesus' earthly work, it must be the condition not of the kingdom's coming but of its effectuation 'in power' (Mark 9.1).

On that work of Jesus his Son, God set his seal by raising him from the dead. By that mighty act, says a modern theologian,[4] Jesus became one with God. Whether there is a better way of explaining the union of the divine and the human in Jesus, we shall discuss later. Meanwhile, without diminishing the capital importance of the resurrection, it seems truer to say that it was the 'revelation', or (better) 'vindication', of the work of Jesus finished on the cross (John 19.30).

*   *   *

In the gospels the central theme is the dawning of the kingdom of God. When we pass to the letters of the apostles, we find that Christ, for the most part, has taken the place of the kingdom. Why? Because by his death and his victory over it Christ became all that the kingdom contained. The gospel of the kingdom was Christ in essence; Christ crucified, risen and regnant is the gospel of the kingdom in power. He is the truth of his own great gospel. And this is why we may not end our study of him with the gospels: it takes the whole of the New Testament to show who Christ is.

· What is the place of the apostles in early Christianity and what may be called 'the economy of revelation'? Of course they testified to what they had seen and heard of Christ not only in his earthly ministry but in his risen power, and to the wonderful new life he had brought them (I John 1.1-4). Yet in their letters the apostles never thought of themselves as religious geniuses transmitting to their readers their own intuitions and speculations about Christ. They knew themselves to be agents of the Holy Spirit who was taking of the things of Christ and enabling them to show their truth to others (John 16.13-15).

The classical passage for apostolic inspiration is I Cor. 2 where Paul speaks not for himself alone but for the apostles generally. How do the apostles regard what they have to say? They regard it as the authentic teaching of the risen and exalted Lord mediated to them through the Spirit. The Spirit's own knowledge, which is God's knowledge, becomes theirs, so that they can say, 'Our thoughts are Christ's thoughts' (I Cor. 2.16, Moffatt). Theirs is not the disposition but the 'intention' of Christ. In short, Christ through his apostles interpreted his 'finished' work as truly as in his passion sayings he had interpreted his 'unfinished' work. What the apostles receive through the Spirit from the living Christ who speaks in them (II Cor. 13.2) is revelation from on high.

We cannot here elaborate on all the apostles' Spirit-given teaching about Christ or the tremendous titles they apply to him. Inspired and illuminated by the Spirit, these men are wrestling with the question, What are we to say of him who has done this great and god-like thing for us? What place shall we assign him in the ways of God with men? What name best describes one in whom God has ushered in his new era and brought deliverance from sin and new life for men? Messiah, Lord, Son of God, the Word made flesh?

Yet, however much these titles of majesty may vary, through them all runs one essential christology, one basic concept of his person. Whether it be Paul, Peter, John, the writer to the Hebrews or the Seer of Revelation, of two things they are convinced, and between them these two pose the whole problem of Christ's person. One is that Christ was true man, bone of our bone, flesh of our flesh. The other is that Christ now stands on that side of reality we call divine. 'Jesus is Lord' is their common creed. All the apostles acknowledge a debt to him as saviour from sin and death. All see in him God's apostle to men. All worship him as the only Son of God.

Finally, we must make our account with the testimony of Christians down the centuries to the saviourhood of Christ.

What is this testimony of believers really worth? Today no argument appeals more to men than that drawn from experience. Now in Christianity this means experience of Christ; for what 'nature' is to the scientist, that Christ is to Christian faith.

At this point, however, some men are sure to arise and warn us against relying on so subjective a thing as religious experience. It is a warning which Christians must not ignore. And yet they have a right to protest: 'Am I really precluded from all appeal to my personal Christian experience? Did not Paul constantly appeal to his? Is Christ's gift of forgiveness to me in the central experience of my

spiritual life quite worthless in settling the objective value
of his person?'

To this they may reply, 'It is quite worthless. If you
claim to commune with Christ, you must not gird at those
who claim to commune with the saints. There is no real
difference between their experience of a saint, and yours
of Christ.'

How do we answer this objection?

First, in *personal* terms, thus: 'If we are not to doubt
absolutely everything, we must find our practical certainty
in what founds our new moral life. This is Christ. Moreover, what he works in us, if we allow him to have his
way with us, is not a fleeting experience but a *life* change.'

Second, in *historical* terms: 'If you tell me that there is
no difference between experience of Christ and experience
of a saint, I must reply that there is all the difference in the
world. Christ has entered history with such a piercing moral
effect as no saint ever has done. Moreover, he has entered
the life of the whole church, no less than the life of the
individual. As our own experience of Christ is deepened
and enriched with the passing years, it brings home a
Christ objective in experience and in the life and work of
the whole great Christian community we call the church.'

Therefore to the question, 'Can individual experience of
Christ mediate absolute truth?' the answer is: (1) Our
own experience of Christ is not just a transient impression
but, as it was for Paul (see Gal. 2.20), a life-faith. (2) Standing over our own experience is the experience of God's
new Israel, the church, down two thousand years:

> I asked them whence their victory came.
> They, with united breath,
> Ascribed their conquest to the Lamb.
> Their triumph to his death.

Having deployed the evidence, we may now essay a
solution.

Down the centuries the problem has ever been how to

relate the human to the divine, the divine to the human.

At Nicaea, in AD 325, the church's assembled theologians rejected the idea of a half-God. At Chalcedon, in AD 451, they rejected the idea of a half-man. In Christ, they said, we have one person in two natures, inseparably united. Rightly they affirmed that Christ was truly God and truly man. But the formula they proposed did not then win universal acceptance; and nowadays it no longer appeals. Today, seeking a solution we employ not metaphysical but moral and personal categories. But what happens when we use this approach? We seem to be shut up to a choice between two theories of Christ's person – progressive incarnation *or* progressive deification. The first uses the idea of *kenosis*, or 'self-limitation', the second that of *plerosis*, or 'self-fulfilment'. But may we not be on the right way to a solution if we seek to combine them?

Consider the idea of *kenosis*. St Paul, St John, the Writer to the Hebrews and the Seer of Revelation, consenting that Christ's story did not begin in a Bethlehem cradle, speak of his pre-existence. As Christ has an epilogue of eternal history, so he had a prologue of the same kind.

In the synoptic gospels this belief finds support in 'the divine consciousness of Jesus' – that awareness of a unique filial relationship to the Father which shines out in the supreme hours of revelation in Jesus' life – at his baptism, at the time of his 'Great Thanksgiving', on the mount of transfiguration. In these sublime crises of his spiritual life Jesus knew himself to be what he really was, and this knowledge was strengthened by constant communion with his heavenly Father. This 'divine consciousness' becomes explicit in John's gospel, e.g. John 17.5 'Father, glorify me in thy own presence with the glory which I had with thee before the world was made.'[5] It finds expression in the earliest Christian hymn, Phil. 2.6-11 ('who, though he was in the form of God ... emptied himself (*heauton ekenosen*), taking the form of a servant'). It is demanded by the adoring faith of the church, as in the greatest of all Christian hymns:

> Thou art the King of glory, O Christ.
> Thou art the everlasting Son of the Father.

If there was such an eternal prologue to Christ's story, then there must have been for him a great renunciation 'outside the walls of the world'. His sacrifice must have begun before the Son of God entered it. When he became man, he must somehow have limited himself.

But does not such *kenosis* derogate from his divinity? No, God is God when he stoops no less than when he reigns. In becoming man the Son of God renounced the exercise of divine powers, so that on earth he might live within the limitations belonging to us mortal men. If the objector says that such doctrine conflicts with the immutability of God, we may answer that an infinite which could not reduce itself to the finite world would, by this very inability, be reduced to finitude. If it be objected that the doctrine involves cosmic chaos ('What was happening to the rest of the universe when Christ the creative Word was self-emptied?'), we may answer that the New Testament does *not* teach that the universe was created by the Son. Criticize the doctrine as we will, we seem unable to dispense with it. Show it the back door, and it will return through the window.

What is the advantage of the doctrine? It gives us a Christ – a doctrine of his person – untroubled by the limitations and ignorances of the incarnate Christ. He consented not to know with a nescience divinely wise. By an act of love's omnipotence, he set aside the style of a God and took a servant's form.

The *dis*advantage of this *kenosis* doctrine is that it leaves us with a humbled God when we need also a royal and redeeming one. Therefore, to arrive at the truth of Christ's person, hand in hand with the idea of *kenosis* (self-limitation) must go the idea of *plerosis* (self-fulfilment).

In man's religious experience we can trace two vertical

and personal movements: God seeking man, and man in turn responding obediently to this revelation of God's grace. Apply these two movements to Christ. Think of his person in terms not of two natures (as they did at Chalcedon) but of a union of these two personal movements. In the life of Christ the two movements – perfect revelation and perfect religion – were united, involuted. As Christ's personal history enlarged and ripened by every earthly experience, and as he was always found equal to every crisis, the latent Godhead became ever mightier in his life's interior. The more Christ laid down his life, the more he gained his divine soul. He worked out the salvation he was, and moved by his history *to* that supernatural world *in* which he moved by his nature. And the life culminated in the perfection of his own soul and of our salvation in the cross, the resurrection and the glory.

So understood, the story of Christ's life on earth becomes the story of his recovery by moral conquest of that mode of being from which, by a tremendous moral act, he came. Was it not something like this that the early Christians were seeking to say in the hymn preserved in Phil. 2.6-11? Such an account of Christ's person does full justice to the moral side of his human life. Though his relation to his heavenly Father was immediate and unbroken –

> No one knows the Son except the Father
> And no one knows the Father except the Son (Matt. 11.27) –

he had yet no immunity from the moral law that we must earn our greatest legacies and by toil and conflict appropriate our best gifts.

A word by way of postscript.

To know a person fully, you must first 'love him, ere to you he will seem worthy of your love'. Down the centuries adoration or worship no less than thinking and reflection has ever helped men to discover 'the truth as it is in Jesus'. In other words, if what the New Testament documents and the creeds of the church affirm about Christ is to be accepted, there is needed a personal response to the challenge with which God confronts us in his Son.

Of course to the natural man, in his pride of intellect, this is nonsense. He supposes that the mystery of Christ's person can be solved intellectually, without any self-commitment to him. Experience shows him to be mistaken. Take the natural man's approach, and Christ will stay for you an enigma. Only faith and love know who he really is; and Christian faith is the decision to commit your whole soul and future to the confidence that Christ is not an illusion but the reality of God.[6]

NOTES

1. The finest answer to this view was James Denney's *Jesus and the Gospel*, 1908.

2. Ernst Fuchs, *Bemerkungen zur Gleichnisauslegung*; 1954.

3. C. W. F. Smith, *The Jesus of the Parables*, Westminster Press, Philadelphia 1948, ch. 8.

4. W. Pannenberg, *Jesus – God and Man*, SCM Press 1968.

5. On the 'divine consciousness of Jesus' see Vincent Taylor, *The Person of Christ*, Macmillan 1958, pp. 156-181.

6. Those who know P. T. Forsyth's masterpiece, *The Person and Place of Jesus Christ*, will know at once how deeply in this chapter I am indebted to him.

PART THREE

14

The Holy Spirit

'Now, Smith', said the Scottish professor to the divinity student, 'Let us hear your essay on the Holy Spirit.' 'Sir,' began Smith diffidently, 'I fear I know very little about the Holy Spirit.' 'That makes two of us,' replied the professor.

If only all our theologians were as honest as this one! Some would appear to dispense with the Spirit altogether. In this category belong Dr John Robinson and the members of the 'Honest to God' movement, since they apparently feel no need for 'the dimension of the supernatural' – the beyond in our midst – which is what the Holy Spirit stands for.[1]

'Flat-earthers' they have been nicknamed, that is, men who, by reducing the vertical to the horizontal, tend to turn theology into anthropology. Karl Barth was once asked his opinion of them. When I am in a conciliatory mood, he is said to have replied, I call them 'flat-tyre' theologians. The *pneuma*, which is the Greek word for both 'air' and 'spirit', has gone out of their theology; and when the pneuma has gone out of a tyre, there is likely to be an accident.[2]

In such concessions to 'the spirit of the age' how far our modern 'flat-earthers' have departed from the Spirit (with a capital S) of whom the apostles speak!

In 1931 Principal David Cairns of Aberdeen wrote thus to an Anglican friend:

> What has grown on me of late years is the very great place that the coming of the Spirit has in the Apostolic writings.
>
> If you come to them with really fresh eyes, you can't help seeing that they place enormous importance on this as something new, a kind of 'wireless' between earth and heaven that was not there before! Because of this *medium* it was possible for every Christian Church to be a kind of replica of the Galilean circle, with the living Christ still in the midst, messages continually coming and going.[3]

'This medium', 'a kind of wireless between heaven and earth', 'the living Christ still in the midst', 'messages continually coming and going' – do not these phrases admirably describe the experience of the apostolic church as portrayed in Acts and in the epistles? Christ's promises to his followers had been fulfilled: the Spirit was glorifying Christ, taking what was his and declaring it to them (John 16.12-15): they were receiving 'power from on high' (Acts 1.8). But, by the same token, does not the passage pinpoint one capital reason for the impotence of the institutional church today, and underline its need to hark back to the apostolic springs of power – that power which enabled the young church, in three momentous decades, to carry the gospel from Jerusalem to Rome?

Let us therefore turn back and hear what the Bible has to say about the Spirit of God.

When you and I sing in church, 'Breathe on me, Breath of God' or 'I feel the winds of God today', we are speaking of the Spirit as the Bible does. The Hebrew word for 'spirit' is *ruach*, the Greek *pneuma*. Both signify 'air in motion', be it 'wind' or 'breath'. Something in the physical world – wind ruffling the water's surface or the breath of a living creature – symbolizes that incorporeal element in man we call his 'spirit'. Then this word 'spirit' is applied to a supernatural power man knows to be working in himself and in the world and believes to be divine. The Holy Spirit is the wind or breath of the Almighty, who energizes in creation (Gen. 1.2), works in history, activates the life of man.

The Holy Spirit

In the Old Testament the Spirit stands chiefly for the vital energy of the divine nature. The creative force of the world, the Spirit is in men the source of abnormal skill, prophetic inspiration, and moral purity. But, as yet, the Spirit appears to work individually, spasmodically, impermanently; and later prophets like Second Isaiah, Ezekiel and Joel look forward to a blessed future when God's Spirit will not only revivify his chosen people (Ezek. 37) and empower the Lord's Servant for his work (Isa. 42.1; 61.1) but be outpoured on all mankind (Joel 2.28ff.).

Turn to the New Testament and you find these prophecies beginning to be fulfilled, and first in the Messiah Jesus.

Active in his birth (Luke 1.35), the Spirit at his baptism equips Jesus for his work (Mark 1.10) before driving him out into the wilderness to be tempted (Mark 1.12). His mission in Nazareth begins with the claim that 'the Spirit of the Lord is upon me' (Luke 4.18; Isa. 61.1). The Spirit enables him to drive out devils, heal the sick, and speak with unheard-of authority. At supreme hours in his ministry he 'exults' in the Holy Spirit (Luke 10.21). The Spirit is the source of his unique communion with Abba Father, as also of his openness to the needs of his fellow-men.

So we may follow Jesus in his Spirit-led progress from Galilee to Judea and to that passion in which his ministry was consummated. What was the Spirit doing when Jesus agonized in Gethsemane and at last hung on the cross? He was enabling Jesus to drink 'the cup' his Father had given him to drink. He was causing a Roman centurion and a penitent thief to glimpse, however dimly, who this man was that had been crucified.

No less, said the early Christians, was the Holy Spirit at work in the miracle of the resurrection. Listen to this piece of pre-Pauline Christian tradition which Paul quotes in Rom. 1.3f.:

> On the human level, he (Christ) was born of David's stock,

but on the level of the spirit – the Holy Spirit – he was declared
Son of God by a mighty act in that he rose from the dead (NEB).

Besides predicting his own triumph over death, Jesus
had promised that the Spirit, incarnate in himself, would
soon indwell his followers (John 14.17), and the 'fire' he
came to cast on earth, would be kindled (Luke 12.49f.).
On the Day of Pentecost (Acts 2) it all began to happen.
Suddenly his followers knew themselves filled with the
same power which had been in Jesus and was now for ever
inseparable from him. The effect was to fuse a motley
crowd of individuals into a fellowship – a *koinonia* – in
which they were caught up into the life of their risen and
ascended Lord.

Rightly have scholars sub-titled the Book of Acts 'the
gospel of the Holy Spirit'; for he, rather than any apostle,
is the chief actor in it. Ever he is the Spirit of Christ who
comes to men when they enter the new community of which
Christ is the living head. This Spirit is the fount and
source of their 'conquering, new-born joy' as of their
'boldness' (*parrhesia* 'glad fearlessness'); and not seldom
they speak as if the Spirit were not a thing but a person.
Peter accuses Ananias of 'lying to the Holy Spirit' (Acts
5.3). When the church meets in council at Jerusalem to
confer about the admission of Gentiles, its leaders say,
'It seemed good to the Holy Spirit and to us' (15.28). When
Paul and Timothy are journeying through Phrygia and
Galatia, 'the Holy Spirit forbids them' to preach the gospel
in Asia (16.6). And so on.

All the apostolic writers – John, Peter, the writer to
the Hebrews, John the Seer of Patmos etc. – attest the
reality of the Spirit in the life of the church. But in the
New Testament the theologian *par excellence* of the
Spirit is St Paul. (His key chapters are Rom. 8; I Cor. 2 and
12-14; II Cor. 3 and Gal. 5.)

For the apostle, the Spirit is God in Christ now at work
among his people. To be 'in Christ' is the same as to be
'in the Spirit'. (Paul does not confuse Christ and the Spirit,

but, experientially, they are one.) And how varied are the roles the Holy Spirit plays in Paul's theology! – illuminator, bestower, uniter, inspirer, enabler, assurer – he is all these in one.

It is the Spirit who so illuminates apostles that they are able to know God's 'mind' or purpose in Christ (I Cor. 2). The Spirit it is who bestows all spiritual gifts (I Cor. 12), binds men and women together in Christian fellowship (Phil. 2.1; II Cor. 13.14), and inspires them to cry 'Abba Father' (Rom. 8.15f.). For it is through the Holy Spirit that 'God's love floods our hearts' (Rom. 5.5); and if Christian lives manifest 'love, joy, peace' and all the other virtues, they are the Spirit's 'fruit' (Gal. 5.22f.).

Always for Paul the Spirit means God not only as a presence *in* man but as a power coming down *from above*, so that in Rom. 8.26f. Christian prayer is conceived as the divine within us appealing to the divine above us:

> The Spirit comes to the aid of our weakness. We do not even know how we ought to pray, but through our inarticulate groans the Spirit himself is pleading for us, and God who searches our inmost being knows what the Spirit means, because he pleads for God's people in God's own way (NEB).

Moreover, as it was the Spirit of God who raised Christ from the dead (Rom. 8.11), so that Spirit, indwelling Christian hearts, is the first instalment and guarantee (*arrabōn*) of the heavenly glory God has in store for those who love him (II Cor. 1.22; 5.5; Eph. 1.14).

Such is the New Testament doctrine of the Spirit as expounded by the church's first and greatest theologian. Others like St Peter and St John were to endorse and elaborate it. And, as the Bible began with the Spirit of God brooding like a dove over the formless deep (Gen. 1.2), so it ends with the evangelic challenge of Christ's church: 'And the Spirit and the Bride say "Come!"' (Rev. 22.17). Not inaptly has the Bible been called 'the Book of the Holy Spirit'.

*   *   *

We cannot here follow the fortunes of the Holy Spirit down succeeding Christian centuries. The story, to speak generally, has often been one of his temporary eclipse to be followed by his glad re-discovery. Sometimes men have so confined the Spirit's sphere as to see in him merely the supernatural operator in the sacraments. Sometimes, alas, they have acted not unlike those disciples Paul met at Ephesus who had never even heard that there was a Holy Spirit. Then, in such seasons of spiritual dearth, providence has raised up men to recall their fellows to the ancient source of power, and the Holy Spirit has again come into his own. Such a time, Protestants believe, was the Reformation.

Chief among the enemies of the Spirit have been legalism, formalism, and scholasticism; and when these have lain like black frosts on the church, men like George Fox and John Wesley have risen up to restore the Holy Spirit to his proper place in the Christian scheme as 'the life of God in the soul of man'.[5]

One Christian truth, often forgotten, is that God is the God of nature as well as of grace: for creation and redemption are not competing categories but intertwining activities of the same God. Accordingly, in our times men like Charles Raven and Teilhard de Chardin have stressed the Spirit's work in the *creative* as well as the inspirational energies of the Godhead, thus presenting, as Paul did in Colossians, a Christ-centred view of the universe.

How fares it with the Holy Spirit today?

In spite of our contemporary 'flat-earthers', there are not lacking signs that the church is harking back to New Testament springs of power and seeking to prôduce a doctrine of the Holy Spirit intelligible to modern man. Here we can mention only two such signs: the Neo-Pentecostalist Movement, and a splendid new book on the Holy Spirit by John V. Taylor, Bishop of Winchester.

Let us take the book first. Entitled *The Go-Between*

God,[6] it won the Collins Religious Book award for the best book by a British author in the period 1971-73. The aptness of the title is evident if we recall David Cairns's description of the Holy Spirit as a divine 'medium' – or 'kind of wireless' – between heaven and earth.

Taylor's approach is by way of what may be called a natural theology of the Holy Spirit. The essence of religion, as Otto reminded us, lies in *awe* – in our response to the utter holiness and otherness of God, of which Isaiah's experience in the temple (Isa. 6) is perhaps the classic example. But, says Taylor, such 'numinous experiences' are not confined to holy places. They come to us in all sorts of places, in multitude and in solitude, to groups of people as at Pentecost or to individuals like Moses in the Midian desert.

The object which evokes such experiences – Taylor calls them 'annunciations' – may be a 'common bush afire with God'. No less it may be—

> a sunset-touch,
> A fancy from a flower-bell, someone's death.[7]

It commands our attention, sets up a *rapport* between us and it. We experience a heightened sense of awareness, not of our own creating. A presence breaks in on us, and we feel, like Jacob at Bethel, that God is in this place, and we knew it not. Moreover, such encounters, whether individually or corporately experienced, often prove turning-points in our lives. In his vision of the burning bush God confronts Moses with his inescapable call to rescue his people from Egyptian bondage; the heroism and serene faith of the dying Stephen shake Saul the persecutor to the very core, with consequences of great moment for Christendom; the statue of a negro boy at Colmar meets Albert Schweitzer's gaze, and the sight of that sad, suffering face sends that greatly-gifted man to Africa ...

If these encounters have such power, something – or rather someone – must be at work in them. What makes a bush, or a dying man, or a statue come to life and become a presence to which we surrender ourselves? The first step was not ours. In every such encounter there has been an anonymous third party, acting as Go-Between, and setting up a current of communication between the thing or person and ourselves. And always the effect is to bring this object into a personal relationship with ourselves, to turn an 'it' into a 'thou'.

So (says Taylor) Christians find it natural to give a personal name to this current of communication, this invisible Go-Between. They call him the Holy Spirit, the Spirit of God. They say it is the Spirit which dominated the man Jesus and possessed his friends from the Day of Pentecost onwards. Every time (he concludes) you and I experience this unexpected awareness towards some creature and feel this current of communication between us, we are touched by something that comes from the fiery heart of the divine love, the eternal gaze of the Father towards the Son, of the Son towards the Father.

So the Holy Spirit remains today. Between us and the other man, making us mutually aware, stands this invisible third person. Supremely he opens our eyes to Christ – the living Christ – but he also opens them to our brothers in Christ at their point of need. Of course he is the comforter or strengthener; but his empowering of us is not so much by way of making us supernaturally strong as by unsealing our eyes to God's presence in his world and to the revelation of his grace in Jesus Christ.

In the New Testament the Spirit is both enabler and enlightener. If Taylor helps us to understand the Spirit as the opener of our eyes to spiritual reality, the Neo-Pentecostals (to whom we now turn) would have us rediscover in the Spirit the cure for Christianity's lost *power*.

Neo-Pentecostalism, as it is properly called, really began with a religious revival among American negroes about the beginning of this century. In a few decades the

Pentecostals had spread over the Americas and into Europe and Africa, infiltrating Roman Catholicism as well as the Protestant churches. Today Pentecostals are to be found in nearly every part of the world. They hold to the verbal inerrancy of the Bible, engage in divine healing, and almost out-Puritan the Puritans in their moral standards. And their aim? To defrost God's frozen people and revive a moribund Western Christianity by restoring the Holy Spirit to his rightful place in the church. To this end, in their services they introduce 'charismatic worship', with full scope for 'prophecy' and 'speaking with tongues', as well as healing by prayer and laying on of hands.

The thing which chiefly distinguishes them from evangelical Christians generally is their insistence that the normal and necessary sign of possession by the Holy Spirit is the capacity to 'speak in tongues' (glossolaly). For them, what we call conversion is not enough: only the first stage, it must be followed later by a second blessing called 'baptism in the Holy Spirit', and evidenced by the gift of 'tongues'. It is this experience, they believe, which really equips and empowers the converted man for Christian service.

So much by way of brief summary. That Pentecostalism has already revitalized many churches in our time and proved itself able, as someone has put it, to 'relax stiff-necked Pharisees and change social butterflies into spiritual dynamos', is not to be disputed; and so eminent an ecumenical churchman as John Mackay of Princeton is on record as saying, 'If it is a choice between the uncouth life of the Pentecostals and the aesthetic death of the older churches, I for one choose life.'[8]

How shall we judge the whole Pentecostal movement? Christians who are not Pentecostals will find it hard to believe that *the* sign of having the Spirit is the ability to speak in unintelligible tongues, however cathartic the Pentecostals may claim this spiritual exercise to be. They will query the doctrine of 'baptism in the Holy Spirit', asking, 'How can faith in Christ, the sole Lord and saviour of men, be a half-way house where the believer receives new life, yet apparently not enough to enable him to witness and serve?' Remembering what happened in the church at Corinth, they will point out that 'charismatic activities' can be *divisive*, producing spiritual pride among those possessing the gift of tongues along with an inferiority complex among those who lack them, and so creating two kinds of believers in a congregation. Nor, with Paul at their back, will they easily be persuaded that the more extraordinary gifts of the Spirit like 'prophecy'[9] and 'tongues' are to be preferred to more ordinary ones like teaching, administration and practical Christian charity.

What then may be set on the credit side of Pentecostalism? To begin with, they are not 'flat-earthers' but men bent on restoring 'the Lord and giver of life' (as the Nicene Creed calls the Spirit) to his true place in Christianity.

Next, Pentecostalism is a protest against an overly 'cerebral Christianity' whose chief appeal is to man's intellect and which does not minister to his whole personality. For the Pentecostals, correspondence of sentiments matters more than (as they might put it) theological argument produced in 'the cold storage of a refrigerating mind'. God, they remind us, reaches down and possesses us in the depth of our being more than in our reasoning mind. 'The heart has reasons unknown to reason' (Pascal).

Third, if we suppose most Pentecostals to be morally unstable or emotionally-deprived persons, we had better think again. Careful psychological studies made by the American Presbyterian churches have shown that they are generally well-adjusted and productive members of society.

Finally, the dominical test: 'By their fruits ye shall know them.' The Pentecostals have done much to promote warmer Christian fellowship, to bridge the gulf between rich and poor, to revive jaded ministries, and to bring new life to half-dead congregations.

The Holy Spirit

That the Pentecostals have a part to play in the re-generation of our traditional churches should no longer be doubted. Grateful for what they have already contributed, we may hope that they will modify their hard-shell 'fundamentalism', improve their defective Christian ethic, and set higher store by those gifts of the Spirit which are for the upbuilding of the *whole* church.

A word by way of epilogue. Once, long ago, there came by night to Jesus in Jerusalem a teacher in Israel named Nicodemus (John 3.1-14). He was curious to learn the secret of the new religious revival sweeping the land. 'What you need', Jesus told him, 'is such a re-orientation in your life as can only be compared to new birth.' 'Impossible!' replied the literal-minded Nicodemus, 'Can men enter their mothers' wombs a second time and be born again?' Then, as they conversed, the night wind rustled about their place of meeting. 'Listen to the wind, Nicodemus', said Jesus, 'Whence it comes and whither it goes is a mystery. Yet how real and powerful it is! So is the wind of God, the Spirit, and so incontestable is its effect on men's lives. It offers you what you need. Open your life to that Spirit.'

Are we not today, most of us, Nicodemuses? Is there not in that little parable of the Night Wind a word of God for us? Do we not need to open our lives afresh to the Holy Spirit?[10] To keep the mind steadily fixed on the subject of the Holy Spirit, writes Wheeler Robinson,[11] is to open the way to a new experience of God. If anyone finds that the familiar truths of the gospel fail to kindle in him the fervent faith and devotion he longs for, he should ask himself whether the lacuna – the gap – in his experience does not arise just from his neglect of the doctrine of the Spirit, the Lord and giver of life. Those of us who are professionally concerned with religion are always in danger of a familiarity which breeds not contempt but an atrophy – a shrinkage – of spiritual response. Like Father Hilary in Rossetti's poem, we need to keep climbing above our own professional duties to the roof of the church where the winds of God are blowing, that we may inhale for ourselves—

> ... the breath
> Of God in man that warranteth
> The inmost, utmost things of faith.

In short, in this very materialistic age, is there not a clamant need to expose ourselves afresh to the Spirit of God who can revive the springs of wonder and adoration in us, open our blind eyes to God's glory in his world and his grace in Jesus Christ, and so renew the whole church of God?

NOTES

1. Stephen Neill has described the theology of Bultmann as a gallant attempt to make the challenge of the gospel existential 'without a doctrine of the Holy Spirit'; *The Interpretation of the New Testament 1861–1961*, Oxford University Press 1964, p. 233.

2. See Karl Barth, *How I changed My Mind,* ed. John D. Godsey, St Andrew Press 1969, p. 83.

3. *David Cairns: An Autobiography*, p. 200.

4. See my *Paul and His Predecessors*, revised edition, SCM Press 1961, pp. 24ff.

5. The title of Henry Scougal's classic on the spiritual life.

6. John V. Taylor, *The Go-Between God*, SCM Press 1972.

7. Robert Browning, 'Bishop Blougram's Apology'.

8. Walter J. Hollenweger, *The Pentecostals*, SCM Press 1972, p. 6.

9. Not spell-binding eloquence from a pulpit, but charismatic utterance which interprets the will of God in intelligible language.

10. See J. S. Stewart's *The Wind of the Spirit*, pp. 9-19.

11. H. Wheeler Robinson, *The Christian Experience of the Holy Spirit*, 1928, p. 286.

15

Christian Baptism

'I have a baptism to undergo'
(Luke 12.50 NEB)

What is really being done when we sprinkle water on a little child in the name of the Father, the Son and the Holy Spirit?

It is an old delusion, but one which dies hard, that baptism is the rite at which the baby 'gets its name'. Of course it is from the parents – often after long domestic argument – that the baby 'gets its name'. We call a child's first name his Christian one because it is customary to utter this name in baptism. Yet the sacrament would be as valid as ever if the name were never spoken.

Other people seem to regard baptism as a kind of ecclesiastical vaccination – a shot in the arm of the soul to protect the infant against spiritual germs.

But Christian baptism is much more than mere name-giving or spiritual innoculation. When we call it 'christening', we take a step to its true understanding. Baptism has to do with Christ, derives from what Christ did for us, and means being brought into Christ's fellowship, which is the church.

Here is the first important thing to remember about the sacrament. Behind every Christian baptism today stands the redemption – the rescue from sin – which God wrought through Christ on the cross.

A great modern theologian, Oscar Cullmann, has

declared that all men, in principle, received baptism on the first Good Friday and the first Easter Day. Then, he says, 'the essential act of Baptism was carried out, entirely without our co-operation, and even without our faith.'[2]

Does this statement take us out of our spiritual depth? Then let us recall that Christ called his atoning death his 'baptism' – a God-appointed baptism, not in water but in blood, in order to loose men from their sins. (Cf. Rev. 1.5 'To him who loves us and loosed us from our sins by his life's blood'.) It is from that great historic act of God in his Son that Christian baptism derives its spiritual value. When we are baptized, we are made to share in the act by which God redeemed the race, and which, by the gift of the Holy Spirit, he made available for all who will.

More important than anything we do is what God does for us in baptism. Whether we like it or not, we live in a world for which Christ died and rose again. By that act God the Father established a prior claim on our lives. To the existence and continuance of that prior claim, and to the primacy of God's 'prevenient grace' in Christ, baptism offers its enduring witness.

If this biblical theology is hard for any to understand, then let us make it easier by means of a little parable.[3]

Sometimes – though the custom is not now so common as it once was – the child's grandmother, at his baptism, presents him with a christening mug, which he uses as soon as he is able to take his place at table. But, later, a day comes when the child asks who gave him the mug. He is told that it was his grandmother who loved him as a tiny child. 'Where is she now?' he asks. 'She is dead – gone to be with the Good Man Above.' 'And she loved me before I could speak – as soon as I was born?' 'Yes.'

So love comes home to that child as a beautiful thing, an unseen, mysterious thing, a thing that was about his very beginning, and yet a thing that goes with him every day.

The gift of the christening mug is baptism. It is a symbol, as our forefathers would have said, of 'the prevenient grace of God', of the divine love that died to redeem us.

And yet it is more than a mere ineffectual sign. In it a real gift of God's grace is given. To be sure, the child when he grows up may, by his un-Christian life, reject and forfeit that grace. Nevertheless, in baptism that gift of God is really made.[4]

When, in his later life, Martin Luther was beset by doubts and temptations, how did he recover his certainty? By reminding himself that he had been baptized. '*Baptizatus sum*', he would say, 'I have been baptized'. At his baptism all the powers of Christ's death and resurrection had been applied to his life, and they were yet potent to scatter his doubts and help him conquer his sin.

If some find this dose of baptismal theology hard to take, then let them think of baptism in terms of three simple words.

First, as we have seen, baptism is a *sign* of God's forgiving love in Christ and the promise of renewal by the Holy Spirit.

We do not believe that at baptism God infuses mechanically some mysterious substance into a child's blood-stream, as a parent might give it an aspirin for a bodily ailment. This sacrament is not divine magic, but God's mercy, and water is its symbol. At baptism the child passes into the sphere of salvation – comes within the circle of the church where the forgiveness of sins is proclaimed and the Holy Spirit is at work.

So, second, baptism is a *door*. What does a door do? It admits. So baptism admits into the great family of God in which Christ is elder brother (Rom. 8.29).

At baptism, a child really becomes a member of the church – a member *in petto*, 'in reserve', if you like. Later, when we talk about his 'joining' the church, he is really taking over for himself the responsibilities of church membership which, years before, his parents assumed on his behalf.

Lastly, baptism is a *promise*. It is a promise made by the parents that they will bring up their child 'in the knowledge of God and of his Son Jesus Christ our Lord'.

Thus, in this sacrament, the *corporate* nature of Christianity comes out clearly. We cannot be Christians by ourselves; we are members one of another; and we can be saved and helped by the faith of other Christians.

In the gospels we may remember how a paralytic was once brought to Jesus for healing by four of his friends (Mark 2.1-5). Such was the importunity of their faith in Jesus that they opened up the roof of the place where Jesus was and lowered the cripple on a stretcher into his presence. 'When Jesus saw *their* faith', we read, 'he said to the paralysed man, "My son, your sins are forgiven".' Thus the beginning of that man's new life, in respect both of healing *and of forgiveness,* came to him not because of his own act but because of something his friends had done for him.

Just so, God's gift of himself in Christ came to us first through the faith of others when they took us to the font for baptism.

This is why the promise made by the parents at baptism is so important. When they take the 'baptismal vows', as they are called, they promise as Christians so to order their lives and their homes that the new life imparted to the child in baptism will later find fulfilment when, grown to years of discretion, he can confirm for himself the promises once made on his behalf.

A sign, a door, a promise – this is the three-fold meaning of baptism. It is the sign of the divine love that died to redeem us, the door of entry into the family of God, and the promise by the parents that, so far as in them lies, they will bring up their child as a Christian who will fight bravely all his days under Christ's banner until, at last, God calls him home to higher service.

NOTES

1. I say 'we' because baptism is essentially a church act. Except when illness makes it impossible, baptism should always be administered in face of the congregation. Moreover, when the parents have taken their vows and the child has been christened and received into the fellowship of the church, the congregation should be invited, by symbolically standing up, to promise their continuing concern in the child's Christian future.

2. *Baptism in the New Testament*, SCM Press 1950, p. 23.

3. I owe it to P. T. Forsyth, *Church and Sacraments*, 1916, p. 162.

4. This point needs to be stressed. When a cat jumps on a baby's cot, some people believe the sudden fright may affect his personality years later. Yet the same people may dismiss baptism as a meaningless rite which does nothing for the child. So to argue is to make almighty God the one powerless being in his own world.

16

The Lord's Supper

At the top of the card inviting members to Holy Communion in the Church of Scotland are often set six words from I Cor. 11.24 (Authorized Version): 'This do in remembrance of me.' Solemnly reiterated, to the grave music of Paraphrase 35 ('*'Twas on the night when doomed to know*'), at the actual service, they might seem to teach a merely 'memorialistic' view of the sacrament and suggest that, when we attend communion, we go – as Scotsmen do annually, on 25 January to their Burns Suppers – to keep alive the fame of a dead hero and propose 'the immortal memory' of the church's founder. (How can we have a 'memorial' of one who is still alive, still our life?)

Is the main aim and theme of the sacrament really 'commemoration' of this kind?

Go back to St Paul and hear how he explains it to the Corinthian Christians:

> When we bless 'the cup of blessing', is it not a means of sharing in the blood of Christ? When we break the bread, is it not a means of sharing in the body of Christ? Because there is one loaf, we, many as we are, are one body (I Cor. 10.16f., NEB).

'Means of sharing' is the New English Bible's rendering of the Greek word *koinonia*. Now, its primary meaning is not, as is often supposed, merely that of associating with other persons – what our American cousins call 'fellowshipping'. It is that of *sharing something in common with others*. In what do Christians share at the Lord's Supper?

Paul answers: 'the blood of Christ', a vivid term for his death, and 'the body of Christ', a phrase signifying his whole person. According to the apostle, in the Lord's Supper there is set up the closest possible relationship between us and our crucified and risen Lord. As he is the host at the table, so in the sacrament there is a sharing both by Christ and members of his Body, the church – a sharing which seals and confirms the spiritual bond between them.

How far all this is removed from a mere festival of remembrance! This is real communion between living persons, 'the king and head of the church' with his people.

If then the AV's 'This do in remembrance of me' may mislead the ordinary Christian, what do the original Greek words *eis tēn emēn, anamnēsin* really mean?

Fine scholars, so very different as the Presbyterian Anderson Scott, the Congregational W. D. Davies, and the Anglo-Catholic Gregory Dix, concur in their reply: 'This do for my re-calling'. The noun *anamnēsis* has the sense of so recalling a past event that it becomes dynamically operative in the present. To 'recall Christ' means to appropriate him as present reality.

Let us dwell on this point for a moment. Much of the difficulty here is that our idea of 'remembering' is so different from the Bible's. For us, 'remembrance' suggests something which is really absent and is only mentally recollected. To the question, What happens when we remember something from the past? many would reply that we have an 'idea' of something in our minds, not the thing itself. But a pale, neutral, bloodless memory of this kind is not what the men of the Bible mean by remembering. For them to 'remember' is to bring the past vitally into the present, to actualize it here and now.

In the Old Testament we read how Elijah 'gave the kiss of life' to the son of the widow of Zarephath (I Kings 17). When the son's breathing stopped, his mother rounded on the prophet with, 'You have come to bring my sin to my remembrance'. Elijah, observe, has made no reference to her past sin. What the widow means is that the holy man's coming has so set in motion spiritual forces that the guilt of her past sin – which otherwise had lain dormant – has suddenly revived and pounced on the life of her son. (Compare the Samaritan woman's reaction to Jesus' revelation of her past life in John 4.)

Such 'remembrance', then, is not merely theoretical and psychological but realistic and dynamic. The sin comes back out of the past into the present, with living power. In short, to 'remember', in the Bible's way of it, is not to entertain a pallid idea of a past event in one's mind, but to make the event present again so that it controls the will and becomes potent in our lives for good or ill.

So it was (and still is) when the Jewish family kept the Passover out of which our Christian sacrament was born. 'In every generation', ran the rubric for the Paschal feast, 'each one of us should regard himself as though he himself had come out of Egypt.' For the Jew to 'remember' the Passover was to re-live – to be caught up again, by corporate memory, in – the exodus, that mighty act by which God had delivered Israel from Egyptian bondage.

Now apply this doctrine of 'remembering' to the command which Paul says Jesus gave in the upper room 'on that night in which he was betrayed'. We may be sure that Jesus was not seeking to keep before his disciples' minds what they would certainly never forget. What he intended was 'realistic remembering' of the kind we have described – a bringing back of the past into the present. Of what? Not primarily of sins but of himself as saviour, crucified, risen and victorious through death.

As in the upper room Jesus had made the broken bread and the outpoured wine the effective symbols for his disciples of his approaching sacrifice, so in the days beyond the cross they would take bread and wine, as he had bidden them do, 'for his recalling'; and when his people met to 'keep the feast', their Lord would be present with them in the power of his accepted sacrifice for sin.

God has a way, said Jesus (Matt. 11.25), of hiding his truth from this world's clever and sophisticated people and revealing it unto 'babes', to humble folk like those in the first Beatitude 'who know their need of God' (Matt. 5.3, NEB). The American negroes who sang, 'Were you there when they crucified my Lord?' can help us sophisticated modern men to understand what the Bible means by 'remembering'. If you and I 'remember' aright, with something of their 'realism' we recall that second and mightier exodus (Luke 9.31) by which, through cross and resurrection, God broke into history and set up 'the new covenant' – his 'new deal' – for sinful men. The cross steps out of its frame in past history, and we re-enact the crisis of our redemption. We are 'there' with the disciples in the upper room. We are 'there' at the foot of the cross with 'Mary his mother' and the beloved disciple. Yes, and we are 'there' with the women on the first Easter morning at the empty tomb to hear again the stupendous tidings, 'He is not here. He is risen!'

Yet this is only half the truth. If we are 'there', He is 'here', unseen but not unknown, to bless us; 'here' in the power of his accepted sacrifice. What turns the 'there' into a 'here'? It is the Holy Spirit. He it is who transforms bread and wine into a meeting-place with God in Christ. To the unbeliever, the life and death of Jesus may appear as things belonging to a long buried past. But to the believer, those far-off events become present and effective once again, as the living Christ renews the new covenant once sealed by his own blood on Calvary.

How salutory it would be if the church today could re-capture something of the glow and gladness of those earliest Lord's Suppers! Every Lord's day – for each Sunday was an Easter festival celebrating Christ's victory over death – the climax to which their whole worship moved was the Lord's Supper – no festival of sad remembering but a time of glad fellowship with the risen Lord, through the power of the Holy Spirit. When they gathered to 'break bread', Christ united himself with his people as their crucified and risen Lord and, by making them one with himself, not only confirmed the spiritual bond between the redeemer and the redeemed but built them up into his Body. In two words *Kyrios Jesus*, 'Jesus is Lord' their faith found fervent expression. When they prayed, it was for the coming of the Lord – not only his glorious coming at the end but also his gracious coming *now*. And the mood and temper of the whole service was one of *agalliasis* (Acts 2.46), that is, exuberant joy. All was summed up in their watchword '*Marana tha!*' (I Cor. 16.22; Rev. 22.20), which meant not only 'Come, our Lord, in glory' but also 'Come now, our Lord, be host at our feast, break to us the Bread of Life, and build us up into thy Body, that we may witness to the world.'[1]

NOTE

1. On this whole subject see O. Cullmann, *Early Christian Worship*, SCM Press 1953, pp. 12-24.

17

The Christian Ethic

Ethic (or ethics) is the science of morals. It seeks to answer the question, How ought I to live?

Some modern moralists, who find no place for the supernatural in their thinking, derive their moral standards wholly from natural facts. Idealistic philosophers base their ethical thinking on 'a moral law' within us which (they say) carries its own guiding principle within itself, viz the autonomous human will. But for Christians who believe in an unseen 'bigger world' transcending this 'obvious world' of ours – and yet interpenetrating it – the ethical 'ought' comes not from within man but from beyond him – from God.

What then is the Christian ethic? Emil Brunner has defined it in his book *The Divine Imperative* (1937) as 'the science of human conduct as determined by divine conduct'. This is accurate but, for the ordinary mortal, a little abstract and academic. More simply, Christian conduct is our response in living to the grace of God, i.e. his extravagant love to us undeserving men in Christ; and the essence of it lies in a single Greek word from the New Testament, *agape*, which means selfless care and concern for others in gratitude for what God has done for us in Christ. Thomas Erskine of Linlathen[1] summed the matter up in one sentence: 'In the New Testament religion is grace, and ethics is gratitude.' Or, to put it shortly, Christian goodness is 'grace' goodness.

Concerning this Christian love-ethic – and *agape* in the

143

New Testament has none of the sentimental or 'erotic' overtones which our word 'love' has today – three things are to be said:

1. It is rightly based not simply on the moral precepts of Jesus but upon the whole Christ event.

2. It is new in at least three distinctive ways.

3. For its practice, it presupposes a fresh bestowal of divine power.

Our first point is that the Christian ethic should be based not simply on the moral precepts of Jesus as we find them summarized, for example, in the Sermon on the Mount, but on *the whole Christ event* – his ministry, death and resurrection – regarded as a great act of divine love for sinners.

Christian moralists have not always been of this view. Often they have preferred to found Christian morality almost entirely on the ethical teaching of Jesus. This 'preceptual' approach, as it may be called, is, in our view, neither true to the New Testament nor relevant to the world of today.

To begin with, it was hardly the apostles' way. True, from time to time they cite the precepts of Jesus (e.g. I Cor. 9.14; I Peter 4.14; James 4.12) or echo the general tenor of his teaching, as Paul does in Rom. 12-14. Much oftener they appeal to the whole temper and quality of Christ's earthly life. Thus, 'have this mind in you which was also in Christ Jesus' (Phil. 2.5), or 'You know the grace of our Lord Jesus Christ that, though he was rich, yet for our sake he became poor' (II Cor. 8.9 where the reference is to the incarnation); or 'You must forgive as the Lord forgave you' (Col. 3.13: the reference is to the cross). In the same way, St John writes, 'In this is love, not that we loved God but that God loved us and gave his Son to be the expiation for our sins' (I John 4.10f.).

A second objection is that this 'preceptual' approach turns Christ into a legislator, a second and greater Moses, which he never was (in spite of Matt. 5.21-48). To suppose that Christ's action on the world is 'preceptual' in this way is, as Paul would say, to 'fall from grace' with Galatian-like levity.

In the third place, the 'preceptual' approach forgets how greatly human society today differs from that of Christ's contemporaries. It is unrealistic to take our stand solely on Christ's precepts and try to apply them directly to a world which has changed vastly in two thousand years. Would Christ today forbid us to keep money in the bank, tell us to give to everyone who begs from us, and command us to sell our possessions and give alms?

The Christian life therefore is not just trying to live according to the moral ideal held up before us in the Sermon on the Mount. It is behaviour which answers God's great grace to us in Christ.

From this first point follows the second one about the Christian ethic – its essential *newness*.

When the early church father Irenaeus was asked, 'What new thing did Jesus bring?' he replied, 'He brought all newness in bringing himself'. With Christ there came into the world a *new principle of action*.

The dawning of God's new order – the kingdom of God – was the burden of all he said and did. But he not only announced it; he *embodied* it. He was the kingdom incarnate. So in obedience to his Father's will, he went about doing good, mediating God's forgiveness to sinners, seeking out the lost, and at last crowned his life of service by giving it up as a ransom for many. This, for him, was 'the way of the kingdom', and it represented a quite new principle of action.

When a French politician told Talleyrand that he intended to 'found a new religion', the great man replied, 'Then you must begin by getting yourself crucified and rising again'. He had perceived that in Christ's whole ministry, death and resurrection, there was revealed an incentive to nobler living without parallel in the history of religion and ethics.

New also was the meaning, and the primacy, which Christianity, through Christ, brought to the word 'love' (agapē).

Consider Mark 12.28-34. Two widely separated commandments in the Old Testament – one the 'great commandment' (or *Shema*) bidding men 'love God' with all their hearts (Deut. 6.4), and the other, lying obscure amid a mass of ritual regulations, bidding men 'love their neighbour as themselves' (Lev. 19.18) – Christ brought together as the two principles which sum up the whole duty of man. But 'neighbour-love', he told his disciples, meant a practical 'caring' for others which transcended all bounds of creed or nation (Matt. 5.43-48): 'There must be no limits to your goodness, as your heavenly Father's goodness knows no bounds' (NEB). Even more importantly, he himself incarnated his great twin-command in a life of loving service which took him to the cross. Well might he say to his men in the upper room: 'A new commandment give I unto you: you are to love one another, as I have loved you' (John 13.34).

A. C. Craig has summed all up in two sentences:

> The word 'love' always needs a dictionary, and for Christians that dictionary is Jesus Christ. He took this chameleon of a word and gave it a fast colour, so that ever since it has been lustred by his life and teaching, and dyed in the crimson of Calvary and shot through with the sunlight of Easter morning.[1]

Finally, *new in the Christian ethic was the combination of present gladness in hardship with the promise of divine reward.*

This note rings through the apostolic writings – magnificently in II Cor. 5.3-10 (NEB) but also in I Peter 4.13f. and in James 1.12. But the *fons et origo* of this 'gladness in hardship' is the Beatitudes (Matt. 5.3-12) where Christ calls 'divinely happy' those whom 'the world' pities, despises, and persecutes. Such people, Christ promises, are sure of God's reward hereafter.

Moralists may murmur that 'virtue should be its own reward' and that this doctrine turns the Christian life into a mercenary affair. Such cavillers only show that they have misread Christ's teaching. Rightly has Bultmann written: 'Jesus promises reward to those who are obedient without any thought of a reward.'[3] 'Do good', he says, 'expecting nothing in return, and your reward will be great' (Luke 6.35); and in what has been called his 'parable of the great surprises' (Matt. 25.31-46) those whom he says his Father will pronounce 'blessed' and reward, are those who have helped and served the needy without thought of recompense.

The third feature of the Christian ethic is that, *for its practice, it presupposes a fresh bestowal of divine power.*

Basically, Christian conduct is the fruit of a heart cleansed by the grace of God. (The principle of it is laid down by Christ himself in his teaching. 'The good tree produces good fruit', he says (Matt. 7.17), 'therefore first make the tree good' (Matt. 12.33).) This was one of the great Reformation insights, admirably phrased by Luther: 'It is not good works which make a good man, but a good man who does good works.'

But if Christians are expected to bring forth good fruits in their lives, they are not required to do so in their own unaided strength. As they walk the Christian way, they are assured of help from on high. Sometimes in the New Testament this is called 'the Holy Spirit', sometimes it is the living and ascended Christ. It is a distinction without a difference in Christian experience, since 'the presence of the Holy Spirit is really Jesus' own presence in spirit'.

Through that Spirit yet abides with his people the Christ who once on earth embodied the very grace of God. Still, as in the beginning, this Christ (says T. W. Manson[4]) has two hands – one to point the way forward to his followers, the other to help them along it, as they seek to live up to their high calling.

Let us now take up a question presently a matter of debate among Christian moralists, namely, the place (if any) of 'rules' in the Christian ethic. The issue will become clear if we set down the different opinions of two modern theologians, Dr John Robinson of Cambridge and Dr William Lillie of Aberdeen.

There is no dispute between them that *agape* is the master-principle of Christian behaviour. But is 'love all'? May we sum up the Christian ethic as 'Love, and do what you will' (St Augustine)? And must we exclude all traditional moral rules (e.g. 'speak the truth') from the Christian ethic as savouring of law and legalism?

Dr Robinson thinks so.[5] 'Nothing', he says, 'is prescribed but love.' 'There can be no packaged moral judgments (i.e. rules) because persons are more important than standards.' Therefore in any given moral situation the Christian, having first got his facts straight, will ask himself, 'What is the most loving thing to do in this case?' and lose no time in doing it. 'Situational ethics' is now the usual name for this view, because it proceeds by 'situation' and not by 'rule'.

Dr Robinson allows that, in the exercise of love, the Christian may take note of those moral rules, derived from long experience, which can give guidance on what is right and what is wrong. But the burden of his argument is that 'love is all', because only love has 'a built-in moral compass' which enables it to 'home in' intuitively on the needs of the other man.

The strength of this approach to the Christian love-ethic is its flexibility. Love, say its supporters, is always relevant and will always find a way. Its Achilles heel is its individualism. No social morality can ever be founded on such an individualistic 'situational ethic'. Moreover, we may gravely doubt whether any individual, however saintly, can think out, on the spur of the moment, love's right response in any situation.

Dr W. Lillie,[6] a writer on Christian morals whose worth is too little known, will have none of this 'situational ethic'. Love, he agrees, is the master-principle; but there are other 'subordinate moral rules' (he says) which depend for their validity on the fact that they really embody the law of love. In any given situation therefore the Christian will ask himself, 'Which rule of action best embodies it?' and proceed to do it.

What are these 'subordinate moral rules'? Dr Lillie instances those forbidding cruelty to man and beast, or those enjoining life-long fidelity in marriage, besides the duty of speaking the truth. Are not these naturally deducible from the law of love? Even the magistrate's 'bearing of the sword' of punishment for wrong-doers (Rom. 13.4) is a necessary, if strange, expression of God's holy love in a sinful world. So, arguably, may the provisions of the modern welfare state for handicapped children be seen as manifestations of that 'caring' love which *agape* is. In fact, is not all valid moral knowledge ultimately just that *agape* which the creator has implanted in men who bear his image – an *agape*, alas, corrupted in us all by sin but now, by their response to God's grace in Christ, being restored in true Christian believers?

Readers of Lord Hailsham's autobiography *The Door wherin I went* will notice that Dr Lillie has the support of this distinguished jurist and Christian on this question of 'a situational ethic'. In a brilliant exposition of natural law he comes down against Dr Robinson's 'New Morality'. 'There must be a relationship of some kind between law and morality', is his final conclusion.

But Dr Lillie has a greater authority than Lord Hailsham at his back. By the evidence of the ethical sections of his epistles, the author of the great hymn on Christian love (I Cor. 13) considered that even forgiven sinners needed 'packaged moral judgments' in the shape of traditional moral rules. What otherwise is the point and purpose of those 'household rules' without which evidently Paul thought no letter to his young churches complete?

Finally, we think Dr Lillie not only a better Christian moralist but a sounder Christian theologian than Dr Robinson, because he holds that those 'rules' which Dr Robinson calls 'dykes of love in a wayward and loveless world', ultimately derive from an all-wise creator who in Christianity stands revealed as Father, Son and Holy Spirit.

There is one last question which must be touched on here, though it is really one for Christians with special expertise in politics, economics and sociology: What, ethically speaking, ought to be the church's role and policy *vis-à-vis* the vast world of industry, politics and economics in which, willy nilly, we are all caught up today?

In the present sad state of our nation it is a question of capital importance. Today there is much cynicism about both politics and the church. Many who in bygone days would have looked hopefully to the church to produce a new and better society, have in our times pinned their hopes on the politicians, only to be sadly disenchanted, such seems their 'fixation' on a merely material standard of living and their failure to produce an alternative and better social order. So sick has become our society that today many men of affairs,[7] with no obvious allegiance to Christianity, are now calling for the 're-moralizing' of our social order and some new code of ethical behaviour.

Yet if there is any section of the community which ought to be giving a lead in this direction, it ought to be the Christian church; for surely no responsible churchman will deny that the church has a duty to translate her holy faith into ethics relevant to the world we live in.

What is the church's calling and duty? To evangelize the world? To nurture in the Christian way those whom she has thus evangelized? To help and heal the ignorant and out of the way? Yes, all three of these. But she has also a fourth and no less important duty – to be *the moral guide of society.*

How is this to be achieved?

There are some who argue that our need today is for *a Christian political party.* (This is the Catholic principle – as is evidenced on the Continent by the existence of parties calling themselves 'Christian Social Democrats' – though once, under John Calvin, it took Protestant shape in Geneva.)

But is it, in the jargon of today, a 'viable proposition'? Its proponents think so. They tell us that the Bible with its project in the Old Testament of a new national structure for God's people, and in the New Testament, of a new world order, viz the kingdom of God, is in fact a political manifesto. The world (they say) with all its resources, material, social and spiritual, belongs to God, and what God has joined, man must not put asunder.

Such a view, however, seems to many of us both theologically unsound and in practice naive. For (*a*) by the testimony of Christ's teaching no political order is to be equated with the kingdom of God, and (*b*) mere piety is no guarantee of political acumen and public sagacity. Accordingly, most Christians in this land would agree that 'a Christ Party' to take direct action in public affairs is a non-starter.

What then? There is, as Paul would say, another and better way – less exciting but more practical – one by which the church can really become a moral guide to society. It is not the church's duty, say its advocates, to solve the social problem. Her proper task is *to provide the men, the principles and the public which can.* What the church can fairly aim at is to produce Christian experts fit to grapple with the problems created by the materialistic and egoistic society of our time. The church should therefore bend its main effort to producing men and women (preferably lay-folk, since ministers by the very nature of their calling are often ill-fitted to do so) who, adding Christian conviction and concern to their own professional expertise in business, industry and economics, will carry Christian principle and Christian cleanness of hand and purpose into the places where the real power lies and the big decisions are taken.[8]

So best will the church today fulfil its task of bringing the light of the gospel ethic into a dark world and prove the moral guide to our sick society which it ought to be.

NOTES

1. W. Hanna (ed.), *Letters of Thomas Erskine*, Edinburgh 1877, I, p. 16.
2. A. C. Craig, *The Sacramental Table*, p. 50.
3. Rudolph Bultmann, *Jesus and the World*, Fontana 1958, p. 79.
4. *Ethics and the Gospel*, SCM Press 1960, p. 68.
5. J. A. T. Robinson, *Honest to God*, SCM Press 1963, ch. 6, 'The New Morality', pp. 105ff.
6. See his article in *Religious Studies*, vol. 3, no. 1, October 1967.
7. E.g. Sir Keith Joseph and Sir Frederick Catherwood.
8. Readers will find a masterly discussion of this subject in P. T. Forsyth's *The Church, the Gospel and Society*, Independent Press 1962, pp. 5-64. Here, as elsewhere, Forsyth is a 'prophet for today'.

18

'Jesus is Lord'

(Rom. 10.7; I Cor. 12.3; Phil. 2.11)

As the young man stepped past us on to the beach among the holiday-makers on a sunny summer afternoon, we saw inscribed in large letters on his sweat-shirt the words: 'Jesus is my Lord'. It gave us quite a start ...

Most of us are so made that we do not find it easy to speak in public about the things which command our deepest allegiance, or move us most profoundly. In church, alongside other Christians, we do not find it hard to sing, 'I'm not ashamed to own my Lord or to defend his cross'; yet here was this lad confessing him in face of the sea-shore crowds. Nay, except for the addition of the personal pronoun 'my', making it his own, his creed was the earliest Christian one known to us: 'Jesus is Lord', or, in Greek, 'Kyrios Jesus'. The centuries seemed to fall away: the lad might have been an early Christian.

'No one', wrote St Paul in AD 55 to the Christians in Corinth, 'no one can say "Jesus is Lord!" except under the influence of the Holy Spirit' (I Cor. 12.3, NEB). It is an attractive conjecture that this verse refers to the declarations which early Christians had to make before the public authorities, and in which they believed that Christ's promise about the help of the Holy Spirit (Mark 13.9-11) was being fulfilled.

Be this as it may, when the first Christians said, 'Jesus is Lord', they were confessing his essential divinity, setting the man Jesus on that side of reality we call divine, according him a place in their devotion which no other shared or could share. Not 'Jesus the man for others', as nowadays our left-wing theologians would have us confess him, but 'Jesus is Lord', this was, this still is, the true and basic Christian confession.

Of course, for the early Christians these two words *Kyrios Jesus* implied much more – implied, for example, that summary of Christian 'fundamentals' going back to the 'thirties' of the first century which Paul 'received' from those who were Christians before him – 'that Christ died for our sins according to the scriptures, that he was buried, that he was raised on the third day according to the scriptures, and that he appeared to Cephas, then to the twelve etc.' (I Cor. 15.3ff.).

Inevitably, with the passage of time, as the faith spread in the wider world and heresies arose, longer creeds became necessary in order to repudiate heterodox views of Christ. Thus our Nicene Creed, which is a revised version of that produced by the Council of Nicea in AD 325, runs to no less than two hundred and twenty-six words. How different was Paul's position in AD 57 when writing to the Christians in Rome: 'If on your lips is the confession "Jesus is Lord" and in your heart the faith that God raised him from the dead, then you will find salvation' (Rom. 10.9, NEB). The whole great meaning of 'God was in Christ' is here concentrated on two things, the divinity of Christ and God's raising of him from the dead. All that is demanded of a Christian for his salvation is an outward confession and an inner belief in Christ as God's crucified and risen Son.

Should not our creeds and confessions today be kept short and simple?

Last century Norman MacLeod of Glasgow, Queen Victoria's favourite, used to put his own *credo* in thirty-four words.

There is a Father in heaven who loves us, a Brother Saviour who died for us, a Holy Spirit who helps us to be good, and a Home where we shall meet at last.

To be sure, it lacks the organ tones of the Nicene Creed and misses out some items to be found in the Apostles' and Nicene Creeds. But it is clear, short and remember-able. As a big book can be a big bore, so a long creed can be a liability, at once hard to remember and apt to say too much where a reverent 'agnosticism' would be more be-fitting. Could not in fact everything that matters for Christians generally be summed up in fourteen words: 'I believe in God through Jesus Christ his only Son, our Lord and Saviour?'

So thought James Denney.[1] Such a declaration, he argued, would 'bind men to Christ as believers have been bound to men from the beginning, but would also leave them in possession of the birthright of New Testament Christians – the right and the power of applying their own minds, with conscientious freedom, to search out the truth of what Jesus is and does, and to read all things in the light of it – the world and God, nature and history, the present and the future of man.'

The ultimate object of faith, he explained, is always God, and Christian faith is that faith in him which is determined by Christ. Now any true definition of Christ must include two statements: first, that Christ is to God what no other man can be; and, second, that he is to man what no other can be. The first point we secure when we call Christ 'God's only Son'; the second, when we confess him to be 'our Lord and Saviour'.

'But what', retorted his critics, 'about the Holy Spirit? Must not any creed, however short, include belief in the Spirit?' 'Nowhere', Denney replied, 'does the New Testa-ment speak of faith in the Holy Spirit. What the apostles ask is, Did you *receive* the Holy Spirit?' (Gal. 3.2; Acts 19.2).

In purely New Testament terms Denney's critics had a case. By the witness of the epistles, the early Christians could not express all that they meant by the word 'God' until they had said 'Father, Son and Holy Spirit' (Matt. 28.19; II Cor. 13.14; Eph. 4.4-6; I Peter 1.2 etc.).

Yet sound and salutary was Denney's concern to keep the ordinary Christian's *credo* short and simple and leave him freedom to think out all things in the light of his belief in Christ.

Nowadays modern man will give no credence to any creed which professes to solve all the mysteries of 'this mysterious universe'. Even Paul in his day acknowledged that 'we know only in part' and 'see through a mirror dimly'. But, like Paul, we Christians today do claim that through God's disclosure of himself in Christ the mysteries which encompass us have become mysteries not of darkness but of *light* – true light, and light enough to help us walk by faith through this house of our pilgrimage and, at the last, 'greet the unseen with a cheer', believing that we are in the hands of omnipotent love.

Facing the unseen world we are like boys at night on the deck of a ship. Passing by us in the dark is another ship, quite invisible save for a series of flashes at its masthead as a message in Morse code is being transmitted. Some of the boys may not know the meaning of the flashes – may even think them some sort of black magic. But the other boys, knowing the code, can decipher the signals and learn that fogs and tempests lie ahead, or, better, clear skies and calm waters. Just so, we Christians believe we have the key to God's Morse code in Christ. Using that key, we can read God's signals. We can know enough to trust and to wait.

Some such creed as Denney suggested is all that the ordinary Christian needs. By all means let those Christians with enquiring minds delve deeper into the theology of it. Theology is just 'faith thinking' – faith giving a reasoned account of itself – and in this modern world we need more and more Christians able to give a reason for the faith that is in them – more and better theologians and even systematic theologies. But theological systems, like other systems, 'have their day and cease to be', and have ever to be replaced by new ones. Mercifully our Christian salvation, as Paul told the Romans, does not depend on our acceptance of any particular theological system, but upon our taking God at his living and delivering word in Christ. What matters is that we really believe what we profess. Said P. T. Forsyth: 'A minimal creed, an ample science, and a maximal faith – this should be our aim.'[2]

NOTES

1. *Jesus and the Gospel,* 1908, p. 397.
2. *Positive Preaching and the Modern Mind,* 1907, p. 127.

19

The Church and the World

For Christians the centre of history is the coming of Christ. All that goes before it, leads up to it; all that follows is derived from it. It is our faith that the once-for-all event – Christ's ministry, death and resurrection – lies in the past: the decisive battle in spiritual history has been fought and won. Yet, if D-Day is past, V-Day – the day of God's final victory over all evil is still to come, its time a reserved secret in the breast of God (Mark 13.32).[1] So long then as V-Day tarries and the war between good and evil still drags on, 'there shall always be', as T. S. Eliot said, 'the Church and the World'.[2]

For Eliot, 'the world' meant much what it did for the fourth evangelist, namely, 'human society as it organizes itself apart from God.' 'Born from above', says St John, Christians are 'not of this world', as their destiny lies otherwhere. But this does not mean that, Pilate-like, they can wash their hands of 'the world' and leave it to its fate. For does not the gospel proclaim that God so loved 'the world' that he gave his only Son for its saving (John 3.16)? And did not the Son himself tell his apostles that, though they 'were not of this world', he was sending them into it to offer men 'eternal life' – life of a quite new quality, life which begins here and now, life which, because it is God's own life, can never die (John 17.16, 18)?

All this relates to 'the world' of nigh two thousand years ago – to the simple society of Palestine where Jesus lived and died and rose again and to the great pagan city of Ephesus where St John wrote his gospel. Yet does the deeply secularized world of the 1970s really differ much, morally and spiritually, from 'the world' of St John?

By 'the secularized world of the seventies' we mean the world which has no need of God – even as a working hypothesis – the world where capitalism and Communism strive for the mastery, the world of 'the permissive society' and the polluted environment, the world of the scientific humanist and the 'hippie', the world which, in spite of H. G. Wells's dying cry of disillusionment, looks to science and technology to usher in a brave, new era in our human history. Lest we be thought to put too much lamp-black into the picture, let us add those not inconsiderable items which must be set on the credit side: a greater concern for social justice, a growing hatred of racialism, a deeper compassion for the handicapped in life's race, a common hunger among the nations for world-peace.

Yet, even when the balance between good and evil is fairly struck, one fact is surely incontestable, that today our secularized society is spiritually bankrupt and very sick at heart. Despite the triumphs of the physical sciences in the realm of nature, the spectacular advances in modern medicine, the astonishing progress in means of communication and travel on this planet and beyond it, millions of people today are haunted by a bleak sense of the meaninglessness and futility of human life. Indeed, where the process of secularization has gone furthest, crime and violence have escalated, the suicide rate has rocketed, mental disease increased almost beyond the power of psychiatry to cope with it, and thousands have sought an anodyne for their despair in drugs.

Does not all this add up to one conclusion – the failure of our 'post-Christian society' to satisfy the deepest needs of the human spirit – its impotence to fill 'the God-shaped blank' in the heart of man. 'Where there is no vision, the people perish.' The wise man's word abides true.

Today, spiritually, 'the world' is like the Gentiles in Paul's day: 'without hope and without God in the world' (Eph. 2.12). Having abandoned faith in the living God of the Bible, men have lost hope both for this life and for that which is to come. Ah, we say, if only their eyes could be opened and their ears unlocked, might they not again come flocking to hear the good news of the gospel! But is not this precisely the service which the church of Christ ought to be rendering them? What then should be her strategy?

One thing is plain. We Christians must not turn our backs on 'the world' and retire into our ecclesiastical ghettoes. For one thing, we cannot: like it or not, Christians are both members of society and, in so far as we belong to a democracy, responsible for it. There is no question of contracting out.

But there is a second reason. As we believe that God is the Lord of history and in the crises of our day is 'sifting out the hearts of men before his judgment seat', we must believe that this process of secularization is to be accepted as of his providential ordaining. Only accepted? Nay rather, regarded as the church's heaven-sent opportunity to tell bewildered modern men 'the old, old story' in ways they can understand.

Before the church lies a two-fold task. Her first one is to be *God's collective missionary to the world*. Such mission today begins just outside our church doors in the semi-pagan society around us, and it ought to be the business not only of the clergy and the office-bearers but of all committed Christians.

Mission may take many shapes and forms. At the local level, it may mean the congregation engaging in a door-to-door parish mission. At a wider level, it may mean the various churches co-operating in a movement for the moral and spiritual renewal of the nation. Or it may mean committed Christians involving themselves in politics and manifesting the same fervour which the Communists bring to the propagation of their godless gospel. And of course every church member, in his own neighbourhood, by the way he lives, the example he sets, and the service he renders, may be a true ambassador for the gospel.

The church's second task should be to *provide a moral guide to society*.

Society contains two elements, one economic, the other moral; yet, at bottom, they are one: the basic human problem is moral. It is for this reason that the church has a right to intrude into the fields of economics and politics and 'apply holy faith to public conduct'. And her aim and end in so doing? The moral conversion of society by the application of Christian principle to the problems of our time.

If the church is to do this, more than mere piety will be required. From her own ranks she will need to produce experts in economic affairs, preferably laymen – since ministers by reason of their calling are often ill equipped to handle such issues. The church then ought to be the place which turns out men able to cope with the problem of 'adjusting gold to gospel'. For as the church's true capital is not monetary but moral, her true business is not to solve the social problem, but to provide 'the men, the principles and the public which can'.

All this poses the question: How ought we to live as Christians in the secular world of today?

When our modern prophets – Dietrich Bonhoeffer, George MacLeod and the rest – tell us that 'Christ came to do away with religion', they mystify and shock the narrowly pious. What they are arraigning is a false Christian 'religiosity', a save-my-soul religion which in face of the world's wickedness would retreat into its own private bolt-hole. What they would tell us is that God is not the property of any religious sect, neither is he a Sunday God or even a churchly one. Not other was Christ while he dwelt among us: charged with breaking the sabbath by doing works of mercy on it, he replied: 'My Father is working still, and I am working' (John 5.17). As it was with Christ, so it should be with his followers today. Not 'of the world', our vocation yet lies 'in it'. We are called to be 'Christian worldlings'.

But here a caveat is to be entered. If our vocation is to be 'Christian worldlings', this must never mean that we neglect the discipline of personal religion – private prayer and Bible reading, the assembling of ourselves together on the Lord's day, the proper observance of the sacraments. Lacking such discipline, Christian worldliness becomes a vain dream.

Here, as always, we take example from our Lord. Christ himself not only 'went to the synagogue, as his custom was, on the sabbath day' (Luke 4.16), but often retired into lonely places to pray, not that he might withdraw completely from the wicked world but in order that he might the better return to do his Father's work in it.

If then, from time to time, we turn aside to pray or meet for worship in the company of God's people, it is that in communion with God through Christ, and by the Spirit's help, we may learn God's will before going forth to do it. Every Christian service should end with the idea not that we are being sent *away* but that we are being sent *out*; that, if our worship service is over, our Christian service is just beginning; that we are going back with God into the world, to illumine its darkness not with our own light but with the light of the knowledge of the glory of God which we have seen in the face of Christ (II Cor. 4.6).

A word by way of epilogue and conclusion.

In the secular world of today there is an empty throne[3] – 'God', says the modern fool in his heart, 'God is dead'.

To be sure, for that vacant throne there are not lacking claimants. Yet never let us delude ourselves into thinking that the 'God-rejecters' have demolished that throne. Parties, states, ideologies have tried, and are trying, to occupy the place of absolute power. But no one has yet found a way to prevent these, or any other human power, from claiming to be absolute other than a firm faith in the God and Father of Christ and that kingdom of his which, through the darkness and confusion of the world, moves to its appointed consummation. Let us then as Christians, as John Knox did in his day, 'give God thanks that we have come in the thick of the battle' and, in the day of our ordeal, quit us like men, knowing that even now the Lord God omnipotent reigneth, as his final victory is sure.

NOTES

1. See Oscar Cullmann's *Christ and Time*, SCM Press 1951.
2. T. S. Eliot, 'The Rock'.
3. See David H. C. Read's article 'The Churches under Fire' in *The Expository Times*, December 1967, p. 86.

20

Christian Paradoxes

> The rule of the road is a paradox quite:
> if you keep to the left you will always be right.

But paradox belongs not only to the British rule of the road but to the very essence of our Christian faith; and nowhere in the New Testament, unless perhaps in the Beatitudes, do paradoxes come so thick and fast as in Paul's second letter to the Corinthians, chapter 6, verses 8 to 10, freely but superbly translated in the New English Bible:

> Honour and dishonour, praise and blame, are alike our lot: we are the impostors who speak the truth, the unknown men whom all men know; dying we still live on; disciplined by suffering, we are not done to death; in our sorrows we have always cause for joy; poor ourselves, we bring wealth to many; penniless, we own the world.

'Impostors who speak the truth' (AV: 'deceivers and yet true'). This profound paradox of the apostle's may be illustrated first in the doctrine of the Fall, next, in that of our redemption, and finally, in the Christian hope.

Such 'impostors' we are when we hold fast today the doctrine of the Fall of man.

The biblical *locus classicus* is the Garden of Eden story (Gen. 3). Enlightened modern men dismiss it as 'a primitive myth' credible nowadays only by hardshell fundamentalists. Apparently they are unaware that 'Adam' is Hebrew for a 'human being' and that the Genesis story is rightly read as a parable of our human situation: in plain terms, we are all sinners and the story of Adam is your story and mine.

But 'sinners'? To many modern men 'sin' like 'hell' has become a non-sense. Have not Darwin and evolution and Freud and his *libido* shown 'sin' to be an illusion? On the one hand, we are assured that evil in man is just a survival from our animal origins which the progress of science and civilization may be trusted to eradicate. On the other hand, modern psychology, as purveyed by the popular press, has furnished guilty man at the end of his tether with 'the scapegoat to end all scapegoats': 'It's in my genes. I am simply the victim of inherited urges and instincts. How can I be held responsible for what you Christians, in your outmoded biblical language, call "sin"?'

So, in place of the Bible's 'primitive myth' men set their modern views about the origin of evil in human life. It is merely an 'evolutionary hangover', or it is the 'hypertrophy' of quite natural urges and impulses. *Homo sapiens* has no need to worry about his future. Before the ameliorating progress of science 'the ape and tiger' in him will inevitably die; or deeper researching into his unconscious mind will sort out man's psychical maladjustments and ensure his future goodness.

This naive optimism about human nature and its cure Christianity does not share. With Christ, it holds that evil originates in the heart of man and is endemic – no mere surface blemish or temporary bad patch which man will speedily get over. In the Christian view, 'sin' is not the inevitable issue of natural instincts and impulses – 'there is no sin in the barnyard'. Sin arises from man's misuse of his God-given freedom. Man centres his life round one particular impulse, e.g. sex, or he makes himself, not God, the be-all and end-all of his existence. This is *egoism*, over-weening self-love, and it is the root of human sin. Moreover, it infects not only bad but good men, making the righteous self-righteous, like so many of the Pharisees.

It was 'good' people who crucified the Lord of glory.

Egoism, then, is the quintessential sin, the Lucifer in man's soul, the source of his rebellion against God. Not a defect in creation, it is a defect which becomes possible because God has dowered man with a freedom unknown to the rest of creation. Hence springs not only the grandeur but also the misery of man.

We are therefore impostors who speak the truth when we say that man's egoistical apostasy from God is not an outmoded 'myth'. Eden is on no map, neither does Adam's Fall fit any historical calendar. Evil in man is a dimension of his present experience. 'Man's true end is to glorify God and enjoy him for ever', says the Shorter Catechism. But we whom God made for fellowship with himself, repudiate our true image and destiny. Every man is his own Adam, and we are all of us 'in Adam', together.

For evidence do we need to look further than the present sickness of society? Are not the seven deadly sins – pride, envy, avarice, lust and the rest – still tragically with us today? Was not the late Richard Crossman right when he said, 'To judge by the facts today, there is a great deal more to be said for the Christian doctrine of original sin than for Rousseau's of the noble savage or Marx's of the classless society.'?

In refusing to abandon the doctrine of the Fall, we Christians are not perpetuating an incredible myth about man's childhood. We are saying that, in parable, the old Adam story testifies to a radical wrongness in our human nature, curable only, on the divine side, by God's grace in Christ and his cross, and, on man's side by 'the expulsive power of a new affection'.

No less do we Christians appear to the world as 'impostors' when we assert that God became man in order to redeem the world.

So it was in the first century when the wise men of the time, the Greeks, counted the gospel 'foolishness' (I Cor. 1.

23). It was no different in the seventeenth and eighteenth centuries for the men called 'Deists' (not to mention the men of the Enlightenment, like Voltaire, who followed them). For them, it was axiomatic that *Infinitum non capax finiti*, that the omnipotent and unchanging God could not take human form without forfeiting his omnipotence or ceasing to be changeless. And to this day there are men – theists, not atheists – who find their reason outraged by the very idea that the supreme Being, the ground of all existence, could enter history and become incarnate.

But is not this to paralogize – to reason falsely? For an infinite Being who could *not* reduce himself to this finite world would, by his very inability to do so, be reduced to finitude. Among the powers of the infinite God must be the power to *limit* himself, as Christians say he did in the man Jesus when 'the Word became flesh'. (And this too whether we accept the Virgin Birth or not. For even if we reject the implied physiological miracle, we are yet left with a metaphysical one – the coming of the divine Son of God into human life, born of a human mother.)

But the Christian doctrine of redemption contains a cross as well as a manger. We believe not only that God became man in Jesus Christ but also in him he suffered to save men from their sin.

Does this invalidate the principle that the infinite God must be able to limit himself? On the contrary, it confirms it. By the self-same logic, among the powers of Godhead must be the power to stoop and serve and suffer. The authentic sign of deity is that, when it blossoms, it—

> ... bursts
> Into a rage to suffer for mankind,

so that, beholding 'that strange man upon his cross', we Christians cry with Browning:

> What lacks then of perfection fit for God
> But just the instance which this tale supplies
> Of love without a limit.[1]

Why then do so many modern wise men regard us

Christians as 'deceivers' and reject our faith? Is not the main reason to be sought in their view of the world? Does it not spring from a too facile optimism, their failure to treat seriously the tragic elements in our existence, their refusal to take a really realistic view of human nature?

When Lady MacLeod at Dunvegan in Skye asked Dr Johnson if no man was naturally good, the Great Cham replied, 'No, madam, no more than a wolf.'[2] Is not Johnson's healthy scepticism about human nature the very medicine many doctrinaire politicians and philosophers need today? What is required to awaken men to the truth of the Christian gospel is, as James Denney once said, 'despair', despair born of the recognition that, no matter how far and high our human technology and culture advance, our life remains self-contradictory in its sin.

Only if modern man can be brought to such a state of 'saving despair', will he begin to realize that we Christians are impostors who speak the truth when we commit our whole soul and future to the confidence that Christ is not an illusion but the reality of God – the God who does not permit the human enterprise to end in tragedy but in the incarnation, cross and resurrection snatches victory from apparent defeat and inspires us with a living hope not only for this life but for that which is to come.

Finally, we Christians appear to men as deluded 'deceivers' when we refuse to relinquish the New Testament hope that Christ our Lord will yet come in glory (Matt. 25.31-46; Rom. 2.16; Col. 3.4 etc.).

To be sure, down the centuries when this hope has been held in all too literalistic ways by Christian apocalyptists who mistakenly supposed that the end of the world was imminent (as in the year AD 1000), it has ever evoked the cynic's scornful question, 'Where now is the promise of your Lord's coming?'.

Nonetheless, the second advent of Christ stands for a truth which Christianity cannot surrender, viz, that the creator, who is our God and Father, will one day cry *tetelestai!* 'it is finished!' to the work he took in hand when he sent his Son into the world to rescue it from its sin. In the Christian view, the long travail of history must include a consummating end. (Belief in eschatology without belief in such an end would be like belief in religion without belief in God.)

History, we affirm, is not just going on for ever – that would be endlessly boring. Neither do we believe that it is merely going round in circles (as the Greeks did) – that would be hope-less and God-less. It is our faith, based on the teaching of Christ and the apostles, that history will end in a climax when not only will God finish his work, but Christ his Son will be unveiled as the ultimate authority and the supreme arbiter of men's destinies.

Some Christian 'modernists' would like to erase the words 'He will come in glory to judge both the quick and the dead' from the Apostles' Creed. The logic of this would be a view of history which does not fulfil but annuls the whole process. On the other hand, if with some biblical literalists, we locate Christ's 'glorious' coming *in* the time-series, we succumb to the chronological illusion that it is merely a point in time, and so turn the ultimate victory of God *over* history (which is what the consummation of the kingdom of God means) into an event in history.

Against all 'Utopianism' (of which Marxist Communism is the supreme modern expression) the Christian faith insists that the end or consummation will be the point at which history – and all in it which is well pleasing to God – will be taken up into his eternity. Against all other-worldliness, the faith asserts that the climax will fulfil, not negate, the long travail of history (cf. Rom. 8.18-21). For, though it transcends all our imagining (as the apostles say – see I Cor. 2.9; I John 3.2), it is the climax at which the human race will reach its last frontier post and come face to face not with nothingness but with God our Father and his Christ now unveiled in his true glory.

Fools in the world's eyes we Christians today appear when, with the earliest Christians, we 'speak to each other softly of a hope'. Yet, in holding that hope fast, we assert our belief that 'the human enterprise' is going to end 'not with a bang or with a whimper' but with the climactic triumph of God in Christ over all evil. For the ground of our hope lies not in human endeavour or in man's capacity but in the character of the creator, who is the Father of Christ and, in him, our Father also. He it is who now sustains the human enterprise, and he it is who will carry it to a blessed climax and conclusion.

NOTES

1. Robert Browning, 'The Ring and the Book'.
2. Cf. Frederick the Great's comment on the preacher who was descanting on the natural goodness of man, '*Er kennt die verdammte Rasse nicht*': 'he doesn't know the perishing human race!'

21

The Secret of Eternal Life

(John 17.3)

What is time? What is eternity? And what is God's relation to them? Down the centuries many wise heads have pondered these questions.

The Greeks thought that eternity, God's realm, was outside of time and that therefore knowledge of him was not to be had from happenings in history. (Were this true, Christianity's claim to possess a unique self-revelation of God would be plainly false.) The true Christian view is that God is present to every time – what was, what is, what is to come. His power extends to everything – past, present and future – as to something which for God is present. Eternity is in fact God's time. (This doctrine is known as 'the compresence of God'.)

Into these metaphysical mysteries we need here go no further. Of one thing we are quite certain. You and I are creatures of time. We experience it as past, present and future. The question is, can we who are thus caught up in the ebb and flow of time, know anything of God's eternity?

St John says we can. Again and again in his gospel and epistles he speaks of 'eternal life'. It is his favourite phrase for Christian salvation.[1] He declares that he has written his gospel in order that his readers may know that Jesus is the Christ, the Son of God, and that 'believing they may have life in his name' (John 20.31). What does he mean?

*   *   *

First, there is a difference between 'eternal life' and 'everlasting life'. Everlasting life means a life that simply goes on for ever, like Tennyson's 'Brook', and to some people mere endless duration, by itself, does not appeal. Eternal life is a thing of quality rather than quantity. It is life of a new kind, life carried into a new dimension, life lived in fellowship with God, life with the tang of eternity about it, life which, because it is God's own life, can never die.

The second point to seize is that this new dimension of life *can begin here and now*. 'This is eternal life', says St John, not 'this will be'. And, again, 'he that has the Son has life' (I John 5.12).

But eternity – God's time – in such a world as ours – is this possible? It is the testimony of religious experience that it is. Were it not so, we would be 'without hope and God in the world'.

Intimations of God's presence and grace do come in everyday events – think of the patriarch Jacob, the prophet Isaiah, the scientist Pascal, the poet Francis Thompson and many another. Moreover, the Christian verities have their roots in our earthly experiences. Thus, though the Christian hope of life hereafter rests upon the resurrection of Christ, it springs from the soil of man's unconquerable hope that he was not merely made to die. Even when ineluctably faced with death, man reaches out in thought to a future beyond it, believing that in his earthly existence his true life is never fulfilled. In the same way the Christian doctrine of eternal life, as something to be foretasted here and now, grows out of those experiences when past and future seem to fall away, and we are caught up into an eternal present.

Suppose you are spending the evening in the company of congenial friends. While it lasts, that time of heart-to-heart fellowship, and your enjoyment of it is steady, all awareness of past and future falls away. You are lost in an enjoyment that is wholly present. When, at the end, glancing at your watch (horrid symbol of mere clock-time!)

you find it is well past midnight, you exclaim, 'My goodness! I never noticed the time!' Precisely: in that simple experience it is as if time had ceased to exist.

Now take a second example. The musician Mozart has described for us his method of composing. He tells how, in his imagination, he could overhear his symphonies 'all at once' – simultaneously. 'I don't hear the notes one after another, as they are later to be played, but it is as if, in my fancy, they were all at once.' He goes on to record the happiness this experience brought him. 'The actual hearing of the whole together', he says, 'is the best gift I have to thank my Divine Master for.'

Now take a last and celebrated example. Shortly after his conversion Augustine and his saintly mother Monica were spending one fine evening at Ostia in Italy, talking about 'the deep things of God'. And, as they conversed, Augustine was vividly aware that they had left time behind. 'Still higher did we climb by the staircase of the Spirit', he writes, 'thinking and speaking of Thee, and marvelling at thy works, O God. And as we talked and yearned, we touched the life for an instant with the full force of our hearts.'[2]

So deep, so intense was the joy of that time that Augustine felt that if it could have been prolonged, it would have been the very life of heaven itself.

Very few of us can reach these seraphic heights; yet here is evidence of how eternity can enter time, and men and women somehow experience it in advance. Now we may begin to understand St John when he says, 'This is eternal life'.

But what is eternal life, really?

St John answers, 'Eternal life is knowing thee the only true God, and Jesus Christ whom thou hast sent.' His Greek is even plainer, 'Eternal life means *getting to know* thee the only real God.'[3] Its secret is a growing acquaintance with the only real God, and this knowledge is to be had by getting to know Jesus Christ who is God's 'apostle', or messenger, to us from the eternal places.

This (need we say?) does not require a university degree in divinity. Let us not decry the study of theology. We need more theology – more good theology – not less. But let us not suppose that we come to know God by toiling through large tomes of theology. Such mental labour will undoubtedly fit us better to give a reason for the faith that is in us. But knowing God is not book knowledge about him; it is heart-to-heart communion with the God who has made us for himself.

'Knowing about' and 'knowing' are two different things. A five-year-old boy may know his mother better than a twenty-year-old one who knows far more about his mother's make-up, mental and physical. So your simple peasant or fisherman may know God better than the theologian who can expound the arguments for God's existence and discourse upon his attributes.

By knowing God St John means making personal contact with him through Christ who is Emmanuel, God with us. One such public and corporate trysting-place with God in Christ is the sacrament of Holy Communion. But we meet God also in the discipline of the 'inner room' (Matt. 6.6), i.e. in private prayer offered to God in the name of Christ our mediator. Then if we will but make our hearts still and let God speak to us out of the silences, we shall come to know him as a child knows his father. The secret of eternal life is growing day by day in such saving knowledge.

The story is familiar, but is worth repeating, how Erskine of Linlathen[4] met the shepherd in the hills and, the talk turning to serious things, asked him, 'Do you know the Father?' The shepherd went away sadly, for he could not answer the question. Years later, when they met again, the shepherd took the first word. 'Sir', he said, 'I know the Father now.' We are not told how he came to know the Father. Yet we may be sure that it was through encounter with Christ who said, 'No one comes to the Father but by me' (John 14.6).

To sum up. Eternal life is a growing acquaintance with the God who inhabits eternity: a life of which Christ his Son is the mediator: a life lived day-to-day by his grace: a life which (as St John is never tired of telling us) is characterized by love of our fellow-men (e.g. I John 3.14; 4.20).

'All this-and heaven too.' For if we may experience eternal life here and now, it is only beyond death that we may enjoy it in its fullness. Then knowledge will turn to sight and in the company of the redeemed will come the full flowering of the life begun on earth.

Is it not time that we Christians thought more about these deep things of the faith than we do? Immersed in the stream of time, busied with 'getting and spending', all concerned to build our welfare states and paradises here on earth, we need to remember that our highest and holiest hopes lie elsewhere; that even now we may begin to taste that eternal life which God has reserved, in its plentitude, for those who love him, beyond the bourne of death; and that the secret of it all lies in getting to know the only real God whose name is Abba Father – knowing him through Christ who is God's messenger to lead us home to him.

> In the hour of death, after this life's whim,
> When the heart beats low and the eyes grow dim,
> And pain has exhausted every limb,
> The lover of the Lord shall trust in Him.
>
> For even the purest delight may pall,
> And power must fail, and the pride must fall,
> And the love of the dearest friends grow,
> But the glory of the Lord is all in all.[5]

NOTES

1. 'Life' (*zoē*) and 'eternal life' (*zoē aiōnios*) mean for St John the same thing. 'Life' occurs 19 times in his gospel and 17 times in

I John. 'Eternal life' occurs 17 times in the gospel and 6 times in his first epistle.

2. Augustine, *Confessions*, Book ix. 10.

3. *Ginōskōsin*, the present tense in Greek, marks that continual growth in the knowledge of God characteristic of the spiritual life. Cf. Hos. 6.3: 'Let us know, let us press on to know the Lord' (RSV).

4. Thomas Erskine (1788-1870), friend of Carlyle and McLeod Campbell, and perhaps the greatest of Scottish laymen.

5. R. D. Blackmore (1825-1900), author of *Lorna Doone.*

22

Hell, Purgatory and Heaven

In the world of art a 'triptych' is a set of three painted panels, hinged together. So in the Middle Ages Christians pictured life beyond death. Pictorially speaking, it was a set of three, and their names were: hell, purgatory and heaven. For us, those Middle Ages now lie for ever in 'the dark backward and abysm of time'; over the intervening centuries the whole concept of the universe has changed; and many beliefs held by Dante and his contemporaries now fall upon our ears like echoes from a vanished world. How much of that medieval Christian 'triptych' has survived the corrosive impact of 'the acids of modernity'?

Let us begin with the middle panel in the 'triptych'. Purgatory (the basic meaning of which is cleansing) may be defined as the place, or state, of purifying punishment where those who have died in grace expiate 'venial' sins (i.e. those other than 'mortal' ones) so that they may become fit to see God in all his glory. Foreshadowings of the idea occur in the early church fathers; but it was Gregory the Great (the Pope who in 596 sent Augustine to England) who really made belief in Purgatory an article of church doctrine, teaching that those who for their light offences were enduring purgatorial fire could be helped by prayers and masses offered upon earth.

How stands the matter today? In the Church of Rome belief in Purgatory still survives, nor has it disappeared in the Eastern churches. For some members of the Church of England, legatees of the Oxford Movement, it lingers on in the idea of 'the intermediate state'. Since the Reformation, Protestants for the most part, have jettisoned the doctrine, because they find no warrant for it in the New Testament. They hold that those who truly believe in Christ go at death to heaven. If they use the word 'purgatory' at all, it is to describe a time or experience of acute discomfort in *this* world.

What has been happening over the centuries to the idea of hell? Though a modern Scottish professor used to tell his students that 'a theology without a hell was not worth a damn', many theologians now find no place for it in their *credo*. Thus Percy Dearmer wrote: 'Hell and purgatory were both bad guesses at a mystery before which our Lord was content with a great reserve'; and of the traditional concept of hell he said: 'All the detergents in the universe cannot disinfect that word.'[1]

About Christ's 'reserve' we may well agree, as also that no brief can now be held for that 'hell-fire preaching' which is traceable in church history from Tertullian to the 'Auld Licht' Calvinists whom Burns pilloried, and which still survives in certain 'fundamentalist' circles.

In the church's early days the dreadful doctrine of 'everlasting punishment' for sinners doubtless owed much to the Christians' understandable indignation at the cruelty of their persecutors, and to a desire to stem the spread of heresy. Yet, later, when hell came to be regarded as a place perhaps suited to one's own deserts as well as to those of one's enemies, the doctrine remained wide open to grave theological objection. Its capital weakness is that it makes retributive justice the ultimate law of God's world, whereas in the Christian view not justice but forgiveness is the highest spiritual attitude.

How then should thinking Christians today regard the idea of hell?

To begin with, let us note that most of the terrible texts

about 'eternal punishment' and 'eternal fire' come from St Matthew's Gospel and are rightly seen by modern scholars to be 'secondary', i.e. attributable not to Jesus but to the evangelist or his source.[2]

Yet if we are justified in discounting most of Matthew's 'horrific' language – he had a special liking for 'wailing and gnashing of teeth' – Jesus did characterize some sin as unforgivable (Mark 3.29) and did refer to 'Gehenna' (Mark 9.43, 45, 47).

Originally, the 'Valley of Hinnom' near Jerusalem where they burnt their refuse, 'Gehenna' had become for the Jews a symbolic name for the place of future punishment. Yet if Jesus used the word, we must never credit him with our ancestors' hell-fire notions of a bottomless pit and everlasting burnings. These frightful fantasies are not to be 'squared' with our Lord's teaching about the heavenly Father who is good beyond all our conceiving, desires all men to be saved, and goes out to seek the 'lost'.

On the other hand, his words about 'hell' may not be dismissed as mere metaphor and explained away. Jesus did warn men of the peril of unrepented sin and the state of mind which wilfully calls good evil. Those who forget this distort his teaching as badly as those who take his words quite literally. There is such a thing, says Jesus, as 'mortal sin', sin which separates from God. For Jesus, to 'go to hell' is the opposite of 'entering into life' – eternal life, life lived in fellowship with God, here and hereafter. To be in hell means to be cut off from such fellowship and so suffer spiritual ruin.

To sum up. The traditional idea of hell cannot be reconciled with the Father of Christ, neither does it contribute anything to a proper human self-understanding. In its images about the bottomless pit we look in vain for the one decisive factor or feature in the idea of hell – *exclusion from the God who has made us for himself.* 'The appropriate punishment for evil', Dean Inge wrote,[3] 'is not to be cooked in an oven, but to become incapable of seeing God, here or hereafter.' This, and not the night-marish pictures of the damned consigned for ever to corporeal flame, is *the* truth about hell. We may not say that such exclusion can never befall a man who by his continual, unrepented sinning alienates himself from God's holy love. But, equally, it is not our business to say who, or how many, will be so excluded.

We turn now to the last panel in the triptych. How are we to think of 'heaven'?

Like hell, heaven is best conceived as a state rather than as a place. Yet, since we cannot help thinking spatially, we may define it as the place where God is. Where our heavenly Father dwells, there is heaven, and for Christians the last end of all their aspiring is the beatific vision – to see God in his glory.

If we would think of heaven as Christ did, the first thing to be said is that it is *our Father's home* and that his house has 'many rooms' (John 14.2). No less is it, in the old phrase, *Emmanuel's Land*. For Christ, the ground of all our hoping, is now there. He is 'our man in heaven' by virtue of his resurrection from the dead and exaltation to the right hand of his Father.

If we ask what the life of heaven will be like, three things may be affirmed.

First, 'the other life then is the other life now'.[4] Eternity does not simply lie at the end of time; it pervades it; and eternal life – life lived in fellowship with God through Christ – *begins now*.

Much of the popular uncertainty about the life to come springs from the church's failure to teach this truth so clearly emphasized in the New Testament both by St Paul and St John. To know Christ is to know God, in a communion of person with person; in Christ, here and now, by help of the Holy Spirit, we may foretaste that fellowship with God which one day will be perfected in heaven.

Second: *when we die, we pass into no lone immortality.*

Hell, Purgatory and Heaven

The Christian hope of life hereafter is nothing if not social. Life in heaven will be a family life – a society of redeemed persons living for ever in their Father's house and in the presence of his Son our Saviour. For the destiny ordained for the faithful is that they 'should be shaped to the likeness of his Son, that he might be the eldest among a large family of brothers' (Rom. 8.29, NEB).

Third: *life hereafter will mean continuance of our personal identity.* This is the clear implication of what Christ said to the sceptical Sadducees: 'I am the God of Abraham, the God of Isaac and the God of Jacob. God is not the God of the dead but of the living' (Mark 12.26f.). It is also Paul's teaching about 'the spiritual body' in I Cor. 15. Hereafter, when God awakes us from the sleep of death, he will give us in the world of 'spirit' what corresponds to 'bodies' in this world. Every man will rise again in his own likeness, his own unchangeable individuality – but *not* in the flesh (I Cor. 15.50).

Reinhold Niebuhr has wisely warned Christians not to pretend knowledge of either the furnishings of heaven or of the temperature of hell. 'We know in part, and we prophesy in part,' says St Paul (I Cor. 13.9). 'Now are we the children of God', says St John, 'and it does not yet appear what we shall be' (I John 3.2). Where the apostles avow ignorance, we do well to remain 'agnostics', content to affirm: 'Eye has not seen, nor ear heard, nor the heart of man conceived, what God has prepared for those who love him' (I Cor. 2.9).

Yet, though we know only in part, we know enough for our pilgrim way, and should leave unanswered the question which the theological inquisitives have ever liked to ask, 'How many are going to heaven, how many to hell?'

Once someone put a question like this to Jesus: 'Are only a few to be saved?' (Luke 13.23). Jesus answered him, 'Struggle to get in through the narrow door'. He compares the way of salvation to a door which God opens and man enters. Without God man's entry cannot be made. Yet once the door is open, man has to make his way in. Nor is entrance easy: it is a case of struggling rather than strolling in; and if some fail to enter, it is not because God is unable to let them in, but because they refuse to enter on the only terms on which entrance is possible.

Thus Jesus rightly turned the question of theological curiosity into an existential challenge. We have no key to the eternal destiny of others except that which we have to our own. 'Are only a few to be saved?' was the question put nineteen centuries ago. Our Lord's answer was – and still is to us today: 'Few enough to make you afraid you may not be there. See to your entry!'

NOTES

1. *Asking Them Questions*, pp. 178f.

2. This is certainly true of the 'explanations' St Matthew appends to the parables of the Tares and the Wheat and the Dragnet in Matt. 13. As Jeremias has shown (*The Parables of Jesus*, SCM Press 1972, pp. 81-5), these are the evangelist's own work. The same is probably true of the apocalyptic 'hell-fire' language in Matt. 25. 41, 45. See Enoch 10.13; Dan. 12.2; Rev. 20.10, 15.

The phrase 'unquenchable fire' (Mark 9.44) which is based on Isa. 66.24 is probably a comment of Mark's (Vincent Taylor, *The Gospel According to St Mark*, p. 412). An agricultural phrase, it needs no allegorical explanation. Any gardener is proud when his bonfire goes on burning.

3. W. R. Inge, *Christian Ethics and Modern Problems*, 1930, p. 75.

4. P. T. Forsyth, *This Life and the Next*, Independent Press 1953, p. 48.